Making
BANK

ALSO BY SHANNON LEE SIMMONS

Worry-Free Money: The Guilt-Free Approach to Managing Your Money and Your Life

Living Debt-Free: The No-Shame, No-Blame Guide to Getting Rid of Your Debt

No-Regret Decisions: Making Good Choices During Difficult Times

Making BANK

Money Skills for Real Life

SHANNON LEE SIMMONS

HarperCollins*Publishers*Ltd

Published by HarperCollins Publishers Ltd

FIRST EDITION

HarperCollins books may be purchased for educational, business, or
sales promotional use through our Special Markets Department.

HarperCollins Publishers Ltd
Bay Adelaide Centre, East Tower
22 Adelaide Street West, 41st Floor
Toronto, Ontario, Canada
M5H 4E3

www.harpercollins.ca

Art by Paket / Shutterstock, Inc.

Library and Archives Canada Cataloguing in Publication

Title: Making bank : money skills for real life / Shannon Lee Simmons.
Names: Simmons, Shannon Lee, author
Description: First edition.
Identifiers: Canadiana (print) 20240507258 | Canadiana
(ebook) 20240508041 | ISBN 9781443469814
(softcover) | ISBN 9781443469821 (ebook)
Subjects: LCSH: Finance, Personal—Juvenile literature.
| LCSH: Money—Juvenile literature.
Classification: LCC HG173.8 .S56 2025 | DDC j332.024—dc23

Printed and bound in the United States of America

25 26 27 28 29 LBC 6 5 4 3 2

For my fam. My whole heart.

Contents

Introduction

Hi there! If you're reading this, you're young and maybe you've got some money. Maybe it came as a birthday gift, or you earned some cash for shovelling your neighbour's driveway. Perhaps you get an allowance or have a part-time job. However that money came into your hands or chequing account, you already know it's important because *money matters*. It's true that money can't buy happiness, but what you do with it and how you feel about it matters today, tomorrow, and especially when you're an adult because money is how you pay for the life you want to have.

Opening this book proves you're smart and ready to learn. I'm really glad you're here!

My name is Shannon Lee Simmons. I'm a certified financial planner, chartered investment manager, bestselling author, and certified life coach. Your parent(s)/legal guardian(s) probably want to make sure I'm all those things. *Check!*

But as much as degrees and letters are important, what really qualifies me to teach you about money are the years and years I've spent watching people, young and old, from all walks of life, manage money. I see who has money and who doesn't. Who is stressed and who is making it work. Who is happy. Who is not. Every. Single. Day.

When I was your age, I remember thinking that someone much older might not understand what I was going through or the challenges I was facing, especially in the context of money. How could a baby boomer possibly understand what I was up against financially?

Their situational financial advice to my generation felt dated and sometimes gave me the ick.

You may be wondering exactly the same thing. How can an elder millennial possibly know what your generation is up against financially now and in the future?

The truth? I don't. No one does.

There's simply no way of knowing what money will be like when you grow up, or even next year. Maybe, when you're 40 years old, everyone will trade digital tokens to buy things. Maybe it'll happen by the time this is published. Financial technology is moving at a rapid pace. Your finances will likely look much different than mine, just as my finances looked different than those of my parents and definitely my grandparents. But here's the thing: it doesn't actually matter. Life costs money, and that has always been true and will still be true when you're a grown-up. Money is hard to manage. That's why there are so many apps to try to help you do it!

So, whether you're using babysitting money to buy takeout lunch tomorrow or trading digital tokens to buy an electric hovercar in 20 years, you will use the same skills to ensure you can save up and afford your purchase.

Why Does Learning About Money Matter?

Even if money as we know it is no longer the popular currency in the future, the life you want will cost something.

Right now, if you want to buy milk, you go to the store and pay for your purchase with money that's in your bank account. Three thousand years ago, if you wanted milk and didn't have any cows, you'd have to give your neighbour (who did have cows) something in order to get some of their milk. Maybe you had sheep and made really great wool. You would give some wool to the neighbour and get some milk in return. Today, we give up our time, our labour, in exchange for money.

Then we use that money to buy things we need now or grow it so that we can buy things in the future. The point is that you had to give up something of value to get something of value. This has always been true.

It's not about cows and wool or time and credit cards or crypto-currency. It's about *you* having the skills to earn or make something of value, understanding its value, tracking it, rationing it, and using it in exchange for things you want today or in the future. Those are the skills that will set you up for a lifetime of financial success, regardless of how the world changes.

The five money skills you need to start practising right away include knowing how to do the following:

Track, save, spend, enjoy, and grow your money

When you are an adult, these are the same five skills you'll put to use every day to ensure financial freedom.

After watching thousands of people try to find financial success over the last 20 years, I know which people are stressed about money and which are enjoying life. Those who don't stress have mastered these five money skills.

Quick Lesson

FIVE MONEY SKILLS FOR LIFE

- Track Your Money (Part 1)

- Save Your Money (Part 2)

- Spend Your Money (Part 3)

- Enjoy Your Money (Part 4)

- Grow Your Money (Part 5)

Why Is It Important to Learn These Five Money Skills for Life Now?

If I had a dollar for every adult who said they wish they could go back in time and give their teenaged self some advice, I'd be rich. So, I'm doing that for you. Time is on your side! This is the perfect moment in your life to start building good financial habits that will set you up for the rest of your life. Don't let adulthood take you by surprise!

Once you know how to track, save, spend, enjoy, and grow your money, life will be good! Learn and practise those five skills today and you won't stress about money later. You'll be ready to take on the world no matter how much things change in five minutes or 50 years.

Are you ready? Let's do this!

A Note to the Reader

Over the course of two years, I conducted research for this book to learn how today's youth is interacting with money. There are a lot of money guides for young adults and kids' books about money, but it's rare to find a financial guidebook for youth between the ages of 12 and 17. I wanted to change that.

I did phone interviews with youth, their parents, and high school teachers who teach personal finances in schools. I conducted interviews in community centres. Over the years, I have also worked with many high school students, with their parents involved in the process.

The four characters in this book—David, Tania, Mia, and Oliver—are fictional, but their stories are inspired by the many young people I have interviewed and worked with.

The Nitty Gritty

Throughout the chapters, you will sometimes see an asterisk, a * noting a new concept. This asterisk is an invitation for you to go deeper into your financial learning by checking out the Nitty Gritty section found at the end of the chapter. There you will find concepts explained in more detail and links to where you can learn more.

PART 1
Track Your Money

What Money Skill Do You Need to Learn First?

To set yourself up for financial success, the first skill you'll need to learn is how to track your money. It all starts with figuring out how much money you make. It doesn't matter if your money comes in cash and coins to a piggy bank, direct deposit to a chequing account, or your future digital token exchange. Knowing how much money you have coming in, and what's yours to spend, is the first step in any financial plan.

Let's begin by looking at how much money you have coming in now, and how much you think you'll have in the future.

The money coming in to you over the next four weeks is called your **Regular Income**. It's money that is yours after any deductions, often called your take-home pay because it's the money you actually take home.

The money you expect to come to you after four weeks is called your **Future Income**. Your Future Income is your greatest asset in life. Without an income, you can't make any of your dreams a reality.

Why Is Tracking Your Money an Important Skill?

Simple. You can't make a single financial plan or budget without tracking your money. If you are saving up for a pair of sneakers over the next two months, you need to know how much money is likely to come in during that time, and how much has to go out, before you'll know if you can save enough to afford the sneakers.

It's a domino effect.

First, you track your money from all **Income Sources**. Next, you calculate your Regular Income. Then you use your Regular Income to predict your Future Income, and finally, you can make a savings plan!

It all starts with tracking your money.

How Will You Use This Skill in the Future?

Everything you're learning here today will still be true when you're an adult. The first thing I always do with every client, rich or poor, old or young, is tally up how much money is coming in. We can't make a financial plan without knowing how much money is coming in over the next four weeks and how much is likely to come in the future. Your Future Income is the cornerstone of all your financial plans today, tomorrow, and 10 years from now. YAY!

What You Will Learn Throughout Part 1

How to identify and sort the five Income Sources

- How to categorize each Income Source by its nature

- What the five types of money are

- How to calculate your Regular Income, regardless of what type of money it is

- How to calculate your Future Income, regardless of what type of money it is

- How to handle taxes if you have side hustle money or a part-time job

- What inflation is and why it impacts you

Once you know how to sort and categorize your money, you can calculate your Regular Income and project your Future Income. Then, you can make all kinds of financial plans. This is just the beginning for you!

The Five Income Sources

There are a million ways you can make money. A million ways to make a million dollars. But no matter how you make it, it will fit into one of these five types of money. Each has its own ways to be tracked and projected. We'll deal with each one in detail in the coming chapters and over the course of the book.

Quick Lesson

FIVE INCOME SOURCES

- Self-employment income: your side hustle, like babysitting, shovelling, etc.

- Employment income: part-time job as an employee.

- Gifts: allowance and bonus income from family. Think birthday money.

- Passive income, investment income: are you already investing? Whoa!

- Government income: income from government programs.

These types of income are very different in nature. Some are predictable, some are random, and some are reoccurring.

You can also have several Income Sources of the same type of money. For example, maybe you babysit and cat-sit. These are both self-employment income, but from two different Income Sources.

You will need to categorize your Income Sources by their nature because you do not want to include random money in your Regular Income calculation. Why not? Because you can't count on it.

Quick Lesson

THE NATURE OF THE INCOME

The nature of the income could be random, predictable, or reoccurring. **Random Income** means you have no idea how much will come in or when. Holiday money is like this. Maybe it's likely that you'll get some, but you don't know exactly how much. If money is random, it shouldn't be included in your Regular Income.

Predictable Income means that you can guess how much you'll make next time you earn it, but you don't know exactly when. For example, if you babysit and charge $15 an hour, next time you babysit, you can predict that you'll earn the same rate, $15 per hour, but you're not exactly sure how many hours you'll babysit or when the neighbour across the street will reach out. So your babysitting money is predictable, but not reoccurring.

Reoccurring Income means that you know when you'll get paid and approximately how much. This functions very much like a regular job.

Once you understand each type of money and the nature of it, you'll be able to track it, calculate your Regular Income, and project your Future Income. Plus, you'll understand how to ensure you've paid taxes and how to deal with inflation. Dun dun dunnnnn. I mean—fun, fun, funnnnnnn!

1

Meet David,
the Side Hustle King

AGE:	14
SIBLING STATUS:	Has a younger brother
INCOME SOURCE(S):	Old enough to legally work but hasn't found a job; random jobs in the neighbourhood
CURRENT SAVINGS:	$20 in sock drawer (on the left-hand side)

D avid lives in my neighbourhood.

He babysits, he shovels snow for the block, and he walks dogs. I've seen him canvassing the area, and he posts in the neighbourhood social media group, letting us know all the ways he can help make life easier for us so that he can earn some money. I love it! David is the king of the neighbourhood side hustle.

A few months ago, David asked if I could spare an hour of my financial planning time in exchange for three hours of babysitting. I was so impressed with his creative money-saving strategy to barter with me that I said, "Absolutely no need for the free babysitting, but I love that you thought of that as a way to get what you need without paying for it."

We sat down in my enclosed porch. It's cozy out there.

"Okay, how can I help?" I asked, excited.

He took a breath and started. "I've got a lot of cash coming in from so many places. I need to know what I'm earning and make sure I'm being smart with it."

"Tell me what 'being smart with it' means to you."

He looked down for a moment and then shrugged. "I dunno. I want to save for stuff, but I also have to pay for my life. I also just have a bit of cash in my sock drawer." We laughed. "It doesn't feel organized."

I was impressed that he was already trying to get on top of his money.

"Are all your pals this interested in personal finances at your age?" I asked.

He thought for a moment. "Some are, for sure." Then he broke into a wide smile. "Some of them . . . not at all." We laughed together again.

"Well, David, I am happy to help. Did you bring your list of questions like I asked?"

He nodded and pulled out his phone.

"Okay—let's do it," I said, and I took a big sip of tea.

David sat back in my squeaky wicker chair. "Okay, so the big question is how much can I afford to save over the next three months?"

"That's a big question. But there's a bunch of stuff we need to figure out before I can answer it."

"Like how much money I make?"

"Exactly. What's your Regular Income?"

He scrunched up his face. "I'm not really sure I have a 'regular' income. I make money from a bunch of places, from all my side hustles."

I nodded. "How are you tracking your money?"

He gave a sheepish smile. "I'm not. I have no idea what's normal for me to make. Or if any of it is even regular at all. That's why I need help."

"Gotcha," I said. "First things first then. A lesson in tracking side hustle money."

I took out a piece of paper and a pen and put it on the chessboard we were using as a makeshift table.

"Tracking your money means you know how much money makes up something called your Regular Income. That's the amount of money that you are pretty sure you can count on in the near future. I usually use a month, or the next four weeks. That way, you can make plans. For example, do you make $100 a month or $500 a month?"

"Does this include the money I already have in my drawer? My savings? Or do you mean just the new money coming in from babysitting, shovelling, and stuff?"

"Another great question," I said. "There's a difference between tracking your income and tracking your savings. They are not the same."

He nodded and typed something into his phone.

I continued on. "Tracking your *savings* is when you count up how much money you already have. This is the $20 in your drawer. If you had a savings account, your monthly bank statement is tracking your savings for you."

I wrote "SAVINGS = $20" on the paper.

"Tracking your *income* is different," I explained. "Income is how much money comes in to you before it goes to the sock drawer. Make sense?"

He nodded.

"So, what are all your sources of money?" I asked. "How exactly do you earn an income?"

He looked up and tallied on his fingers. "Babysitting, tutoring, shovelling snow, mowing grass, and dog-walking mostly."

"You're so industrious!"

He shrugged. "I can't seem to get a job-job, so I do what I can, when I can."

"Which gives us the perfect lead-in to the five types of money." I listed them out loud and wrote them down as I went. "Gifts, like allowance or birthday money. Self-employment income, which is labour you're paid for outside employment. Employment income, a job-job. Passive income from investments. And government grants."

I showed him the list. "Which type of money do you think yours is?"

"Self-employment?" he asked. "Am I, like, a real self-employed business?"

"You are," I said, and I saw him look a bit squeamish. "Does that feel strange?"

"Yeah, I didn't think babysitting and dog-walking was a formal business. I just assumed I was sort of working on the side, but that I don't have to do anything about that with the government."

"Technically, any time anyone in Canada is paid for their labour, it's considered self-employment income. Congrats, David, you're a sole proprietor." I smiled.

He did not look pleased.

"Are you okay?" I asked.

"I haven't registered anything with the government, and I definitely haven't put money aside for taxes on it. Am I going to, like, owe a bunch of money next year or go to jail?"

"Yes," I said solemnly. "They are on their way now."

He raised an eyebrow, and I broke out into a big smile. "Just kidding."

We chuckled. I knew David pretty well, so I was confident a bit of humour wouldn't freak him out too much.

"Let's take a minute to chat about what self-employment income is and how it impacts you and your taxes, because all the money you're making from your side hustles is self-employment income."

He nodded.

"The long and short of it is that all the money you make is technically taxable income, but that doesn't mean you'll owe taxes."

He looked a bit confused.

"Bear with me," I said, "because this stuff is dry, but you need to know it. In Canada, all earned income is potentially taxable income.

It would be the same if you had a part-time job earning $15 an hour at a grocery store. You would likely only take home $12 an hour because the rest would go to taxes, or Employment Insurance, or other deductions. Those deductions would automatically come off your paycheque. Lots of different types of deductions come off paycheques, most of them when you're older. For now, at your age, it's only income tax and Employment Insurance."

"Ahhh! My mom is always frustrated about how many deductions come off her pay."

I smiled. "It can feel like a lot sometimes. Especially when you're an adult. But since you're self-employed, it's up to you to put that aside yourself. So if you get $15 per hour for babysitting, a good practice would be to put $3 (20%) of that aside for tax time and only spend or save the $12 left over if you think you'll owe."

"Do you think I'll owe taxes on this money I've earned?"

"It's unlikely. It depends on how much you're making. In Canada and in each province, there's something called the 'basic personal amount.' This is a tax credit. If you earn less than the basic personal amount, you'll be exempt from paying tax. In 2024, it was $12,399 in Ontario and $15,705 for Canada."

"Okay. So you're saying that I still have to *file* taxes at tax time as a self-employed person, but that if I earned below the 12 thousand number, the basic personal amount, I likely won't have to pay taxes."

"Exactly. You file, but you likely don't have to pay. Plus, you're younger than 18. So you don't have to pay into the Canada Pension Plan* yet."

He looked relieved. "Okay, I definitely didn't make more than that so far this year. But I've also never paid taxes. Is that a problem?"

"It shouldn't be. Because you didn't earn more than the basic personal amount, you don't have to put the 20% aside. If you do eventually earn more than that, then you should put some money aside for taxes every time you get paid. It's a good habit as well. Now, back to tracking your money."

He nodded and I continued. "Step 1. We need to make a list of all the Income Sources from your side hustle income."

David had two babysitting gigs; one tutoring job; and various snow shovelling, lawn mowing, and dog-walking opportunities throughout the year.

"I'm going to give you a chart. You can use it to calculate your Regular Income after today on your own."

I filled out the chart with the sources of his income.

Regular Income Calculator with Income Sources

Income Source	Random	Predictable	Reoccurring	Included in Regular Income	A Predictable Income Amount $	B How many times in the next 4 weeks?	C Total Regular Income	D Tax*
Babysitting Olivia								
Tutoring								
Dog-walking Luna								
Babysitting Sammy								
Shovelling/ lawn mowing								
Dog-walking Max								
TOTAL								

"Step 2 is to categorize these jobs. You need to tell me if the money you earn from them is random, predictable, or reoccurring."

"What do you mean?" he asked.

"Random Income means that you have absolutely no idea how much or when money will come in to you. Holiday money or gift money for birthdays can be like this. Kind of like bonus money."

"I get it. Like, I don't know if my grandma will give me $50 at Christmas. Maybe she won't, maybe she will, maybe it's less."

"Exactly. It's random. Random money should never be included when you're calculating your Regular Income, because we just can't count on it. You have to look at random money like a pure bonus."

"What about my babysitting money from Sammy?" he asked. "I know I'll make $15 per hour but I just never know when Sammy's mom will text me to babysit. Is that considered random?"

"Great question. I would not consider that random because Random Income means you don't know how much *or* when. But with Sammy's babysitting money, you know how much, you just don't know when. Predictable Income means that you can guess how much you'll make next time you make money from that Income Source, but you don't know exactly when. So your babysitting money is predictable, but not reoccurring."

"I think I have a bunch of this kind of income. Predictable, but not reoccurring."

"Tell me more."

"So, babysitting Sammy. I know how much I'll make per hour, but not when I'll make it. So that one's predictable. Shovelling snow, I charge $10 every time, but I don't know when it's going to snow, so it's also predictable. I know how much, I just don't know when. Same for lawn mowing."

"Exactly! Let's talk about babysitting Olivia, tutoring, and dog-walking. You don't think they are Random Income or predictable. Why?"

"I babysit Olivia once a month, guaranteed. Her parents have a monthly date night. It's always scheduled way in advance. So I know I'll make four hours at $15 per hour, and I know when it's going to happen."

"Perfect. That definitely qualifies as reoccurring income. When income you make is reoccurring, it means that you know *when* you'll get paid and pretty close to how much. This functions very much like a regular job."

"Tutoring is the same then," he said. "It's $25 a week for the next four weeks at least. Not sure if they'll need me after that, but it's definitely $25 a week for now."

"What about dog-walking?"

"Both."

"Tell me about that."

He smiled and I could tell this was his favourite gig. "I only walk two dogs in the neighbourhood. I walk Mrs. Rivere's dog, Luna, three times a week. Every week. Rain or shine. Mrs. Rivere has mobility issues, and her daughter asked me to help take Luna to the dog park. So, I make $5 for a 20-minute dog-park trip. I can count on that. That would be reoccurring."

"What's the other dog you walk?" I had seen him around the neighbourhood with Luna, but I didn't know the second one.

"Max. Down on Pine Road. I walk him for $10! They insisted on paying me more than $5, which is wild. It's great money for me, but I just never know when they'll need me. They only text me to take him when one of them is out of town and they just need an extra hand. Sometimes I make $50 in one week! Then nothing for months."

"Pop quiz! What is the nature of that income?"

He smiled. "Predictable. I know how much per session, but I don't know when I'll make it."

"Nice work! Okay, let's pop this all into your chart and see what we come up with.

David's Predictable Income

Income Source	Random	Predictable	Reoccurring	Included in Regular Income	Tax	A Predictable Income Amount $	B How many times in the next 4 weeks?	C Total Regular Income
Babysitting Olivia		X	Yes			$60 ($15 x 4 hours)		
Tutoring		X	Yes			$25/ week		
Dog-walking Luna		X	Yes			$5/ walk		
Babysitting Sammy	X		Yes			$15/ hour		
Shovelling/ lawn mowing	X		Yes			$10/ house		
Dog-walking Max	X		Yes			$10/ walk		
TOTAL								

"Step 3, the last step in calculating your Regular Income, is to tally up how much you'll make in the next month. It doesn't have to be a month, you could use a week if you're working with a really short time horizon, but typically, a month is a good framework to start with. It's long enough that you don't miss money, like Olivia's parents going on their date, but also short enough that it's fairly predictable. It's not a full Projected Future Income."

"Do I just tell you how many times I think those people will call me?" he asked.

"Yep! Let's start first with the reoccurring income. In the next four weeks, what will you make from each of those Income Sources?"

He took out his phone again and tapped the calendar. "I know I'll make $60 from babysitting Olivia. I have it scheduled usually three to four months out."

"That's $60 ($60 x 1) over the next four weeks." I popped it into his Regular Income Calculation chart. "What else?"

"Tutoring," he said. "I have four weeks left of that. Not sure what happens after, but for the next four weeks, I can count on $25 per week. It's really good money. But the gigs are few and far between."

"The gig economy," I said with a grin and added it to the same chart. "That's $100 ($25 x 4)!"

We carried on. "The last reoccurring Income Source for you is walking Mrs. Rivere's dog, Luna, at $5 per walk, yes?"

"Yep. And I usually do it three times a week, every week."

"That would be 12 walks in the next four weeks (3 per week x 4 weeks)."

He did the mental math in his head. "That sounds right."

Into the chart it went.

"Wow, you've got $220 ($60 from Olivia + $100 from tutoring + $60 from Luna) coming in in the next four weeks!" I was stoked for him.

He smiled. "It's a good month when tutoring is happening."

"What do you tutor?"

"French."

"*Très bien!*" I said, in my best grade 9 French accent.

"*Merci.*"

More laughter as we moved on.

"What about the other money?" he asked. "The predictable but not reoccurring kind. Do I include those jobs?"

"Yes! Think about the next four weeks. Let's go through them one by one." I held up the chart. "Will you babysit Sammy in the next four weeks?"

He looked at his schedule. "Hmmm. Probably not. I just babysat for them a week ago, so it's possible, but not likely."

"Okay, I will add a zero for Sammy in column B for the next four weeks."

"What if they call me?"

"Pop it in! This isn't an exact science when it comes to the Predictable Income. Reoccurring is much easier to calculate. It's better to estimate conservatively and be pleasantly surprised, than to overestimate and be disappointed."

"Okay, what about snow shovelling?" I said, and we burst out laughing. It was the end of May and hot. "For real, though, any lawn mowing right now?"

"No one has lawns here! All gardens. I keep posting it in the neighbourhood social media group, but I've only ever had one person take me up on it in the last two years."

"So, snow shovelling is much more lucrative, but we need snow. So I'll add a zero to this column as well. And lastly, are you scheduled to walk Max at all in the next four weeks?"

He perked up. "I am!" He scrolled through his calendar. "In three weeks, I am booked four times in one week!"

"Amazing!" I added it to the chart and turned it to him. "We've finished Step 3. Now, to calculate your Regular Income, just add up all the numbers in column C."

He looked at the chart and did some quick mental math. "$60 +

$100 + $60 + $0 + $0 + $40 is $260." He looked surprised. "So it's $260 for the next four weeks."

"You got it! Wonderful! And we know you don't need to put aside anything for taxes because your income will be well below the basic personal amount this year. So, the full $260 is yours."

David's Regular Income Calculation

Income Source	Random	Predictable	Reoccurring	Included in Regular Income	Tax	A Predictable Income amount $	B How many times in the next 4 weeks?	C Total Regular Income
Babysitting Olivia		X	Yes		No	$60/month ($15 x 4 hours)	1	$60 ($60 x 1)
Tutoring		X	Yes		No	$25/week	4	$100 ($25 x 4)
Dog-walking Luna		X	Yes		No	$5/walk	12 (3 times per week)	$60 ($5 x 12)
Babysitting Sammy	X		Yes		No	$15/hour	0	$0 ($15 x 0)
Shovelling/lawn mowing	X		Yes		No	$10/house	0	$0 ($10 x 0)
Dog-walking Max	X		Yes		No	$10/walk	4	$40 ($10 x 4)
TOTAL								$260 ($60 + $100 + $60 + $40)

"Awesome." He smiled. "This feels great to know, like, exactly what I'm working with."

"I'm so glad."

"So, I just do this each month?"

"Yeah, and then you'll know what your Regular Income will be for the month ahead."

"That's actually really simple, but I just wasn't doing it. I usually just have money come and go. I also never considered thinking about it like this. It feels less random. I can, like, plan on it."

"That's the point. You can plan on it."

"And if it changes, I can just update it."

"Yep."

"Is there an app for this?"

"Many. The financial technology options are changing quickly in Canada. But the income tracking skills that you're learning here are important no matter what app you use. You can also use a good old-fashioned spreadsheet. I can send you the template."

He smiled. "I'll probably find an app."

I laughed out loud.

Our time was up, and David had to go. We made a plan to touch base in a week to make a financial plan to save now that he knew how to track his income. Stay tuned for more of David's story in Part 2: Save Your Money.

CHAPTER 1 NITTY GRITTY

Canada Pension Plan

- The Canada Pension Plan (CPP) retirement pension is a monthly, taxable benefit that replaces part of your income when you retire. If you qualify, you'll receive the CPP retirement pension for the rest of your life.

- You start contributing to this after you turn 18. https://www. canada.ca/en/services/benefits/publicpensions/cpp.html

Do You Need to File Income Tax?

- Filing and paying tax are two different things. You can file but not pay.

- There is no specific age when you need to start paying income tax in Canada. Instead, you're required to pay income tax once you start earning a certain amount each year. Visit https://www .canada.ca/en/revenue-agency/services/tax/individuals/topics /about-your-tax-return/you-have-file-a-return.html for more information.

- The basic personal amount is the amount of income that you are allowed to earn before you must start paying taxes. There's one for your province and one for all of Canada. More here: https://www .canada.ca/en/revenue-agency/programs/about-canada-revenue -agency-cra/federal-government-budgets/basic-personal-amount .html.

Your Estimated Tax Rate

- You can estimate your taxes owing and your tax rate with an online tax calculator like this one: https://www.wealthsimple.com/en-ca /tool/tax-calculator.

- Please note: Some of the figures from this calculator may differ from the ones in this book depending on the year you are using it.

Do You Know Your Stuff?

Test your knowledge with these True or False questions.

QUESTION 1: Tracking each Income Source is important so you can calculate your Regular Income. *True.*

QUESTION 2: The definition of Regular Income is income that comes and goes regularly.

False. Regular Income is money you have coming in after deductions in the next four weeks.

QUESTION 3: Your Regular Income is the cornerstone of all financial plans you want to make now and in the future. *True.*

QUESTION 4: There are three different types of income.

False. There are five: gifts, self-employment income, employment income, passive income, and government grants.

QUESTION 5: The nature of income can be random, predictable, or reoccurring. *True.*

HOMEWORK

Calculate your Regular Income.

STEP 1: List all your sources of income. Include all types of income: gifts, self-employment income, employment income, passive income, and government grants.

STEP 2: Categorize each source by the nature of income: random, predictable, or reoccurring.

STEP 3: Calculate the Predictable Income amount for each Income Source. This is how much you earn each time you do the job. For example, $15 per hour, $10 per dog walk (A).

STEP 4: Guess how many times you will be paid the amount in Step 3 over the next four-week period (B) for each Income Source.

STEP 5: Calculate how much money you will earn from each Income Source by multiplying the number from Step 3 by the number in Step 4 (A x B = C).

STEP 6: Calculate any taxes you may owe with an online income tax estimator* (D).

STEP 7: Subtract the taxes owing (C – D).

Regular Income Calculator

Income Source	Random	Predictable	Reoccurring	Included in Regular Income	Tax	A Predictable Income amount $	B How many times in the next 4 weeks?	C Total Regular Income (A x B)
TOTAL								

Meet Tania,
Employee of the Month

AGE:	17 (almost 18)
SIBLING STATUS:	Has a younger brother
INCOME SOURCE:	Part-time job at the local arena
CURRENT SAVINGS:	$2,500 in savings account

got an email from Tania a while ago.

I'm almost 18. I've watched my parents struggle financially my whole life. I have major expenses coming up and no financial support from them (which is fine, but still sucks). My plan is to work for a full year after high school to save up some money for post-secondary tuition. I will need to take on government student loans and lines of credit. I work evenings and weekends at a local arena and will work full-time there for the next year. I can probably keep my job while I'm at school, as long as I can keep my studies up. I need to learn how to live without spending money.

I replied to Tania by email to see if a parent or guardian would be attending and signing our letter of engagement. Tania isn't the age of majority in Alberta yet (18), so she is considered a minor. The age of majority differs from province to province.

Her answer came back:

> My mom will sign, but she won't be on the call. Is that an issue?

I wrote to her again.

> It's not an issue, but just so you know, this would be considered a "joint engagement" with your mom, so all the information from our meeting would then have to be shared with her. Are you okay with that?

She responded almost instantly.

> That's fine. I don't think she will read it. Also, I'll be paying.

In our first online meeting, Tania looked very serious. I sensed she wouldn't be up for small talk and jumped right to the heart of the matter.

"Tell me what needs to happen today so that when you get off the call, you're like, 'Yes. That's exactly what I needed. So worth the time.'"

"I'd love to get the answers to my questions from the documents I sent over before this meeting."

Tania was all business.

These were the questions she had sent in:

Questions for Shannon

1. How much money will I make between now and school starting if I take a year off after high school?

2. How can I balance school and working while I finish high school if I have to earn a lot?

3. How much do I need to save to offset the debt that I have to take on for school?

4. How to not spend money.

5. How to grow my money.

"Before we do the questions, I just want to check in. How are you feeling about our meeting today?"

"What do you mean?"

"Are you nervous? Excited?"

She paused for a moment. "I'm looking forward to getting some actual answers to the questions I have and not just endlessly searching on the internet. I've tried to answer all these myself, but I really want to make sure I'm doing it the right way."

"Of all the questions, which is the most pressing? Where do you want to start?"

"The first one is good. I need to know how much I will realistically make and whether it's worth it or not to take a year off between high school and post-secondary to work full-time."

"I think that's a great place to start. The way I see it, we need to track your money in a few different ways."

I shared my screen and showed her a document I had been working on while prepping for our meeting.

"You've got different income and expenses for two different phases here. Do you agree with these?"

On the page, it showed

PHASE 1: Still in high school. Part-time work

PHASE 2: Year off. Full-time work

She nodded.

"So, we need to do a few things. First, we calculate your Regular Income, which is your current part-time income, for Phase 1. Then, we use that to calculate your Future Income in Phase 1 and Phase 2.

Once we know those, we can calculate how much money you're going to be able to make between now and school. Plus, how much you could potentially earn part-time once you're in school."

"I've got my T4* and my most recent paystub right here. We'll need those, right?"

"Absolutely," I said as I changed the screen to her Regular Income Calculation chart. "We'll use your T4 to calculate your Regular Income for each phase."

She leaned in toward her screen to see the chart.

"Is this for tracking all my money?" she asked.

"It's for tracking all of your income. It doesn't include the existing $2,500 in your savings account at the bank. Your bank is tracking that for you."

"Aren't my paystub and T4 tracking my income too?"

"Great question. Yes, they are, but maybe you have other sources of income we need to add in here. Also, paystubs track what's happened to date from one job. T4s summarize everything that happened from the job over the year. But I want to know what's going to come in next. Not necessarily what's already come in. Does that make sense?"

"Yeah, that makes sense. Paystubs and T4s track what already happened. What we are doing is tracking and projecting for the future."

"Exactly," I said. "Step 1 is to list all your Income Sources for me. From what I can tell, you have one part-time job, but I wonder if you have any other Income Sources from other types of money?"

"What do you mean, 'types of money'?"

"There are five." I listed them. "Gifts, which are like allowances, gifts from family, et cetera. There's self-employment money from, like, a side hustle. Employment income, which you have. Passive income, which is money from investing. And government income, which is things like tax refunds or government grant money. Since you're 17, I don't think you'll have any government money yet, but you probably get a bit of a tax refund each year, right?"

"Yes, I do. My employer takes off tax and Employment Insurance (EI) and CPP (Canada Pension Plan) but I get a tax refund each year. Last year was, like, $800!" She was excited about this.

"Tax refunds are the best! And also an Income Source for you." I wrote it down in the chart. "Also, can you check your T4? Your employer should be taking EI but not CPP. Not yet, since you're not 18. That will start in a few weeks for you but shouldn't have happened yet. It would be in box 16 on the T4."

She shared her screen with her T4 on it. Nothing in box 16. Phew!

"Okay, great. And, you can see here, box 14 is your total income in the last calendar year."

"Not much. I make minimum wage."

"Living off minimum wage is incredibly difficult with the cost of living so high."

"My mom and I make almost the same hourly wage. It's been really hard. I don't want to struggle with money and be stressed my whole life."

I nodded.

"Is box 18 my Employment Insurance?* So, if I get laid off, I'd collect money from the government?"

"Yes. EI covers 55% of your average weekly earnings up to a maximum."

"Well, that's fun. And you're saying that in a few weeks, I'll also have CPP deducted, so I'll make even less money than I do now?"

"I hate to say yes, but yes."

"Sweet," she said. Defeated.

"It helps to think of CPP as future savings for yourself. You'll see that again when you're retired. It's inflation-protected income for life. Future you can still be excited about that."

"If the planet doesn't explode by then."

"That is true."

I acknowledge this kind of thing a lot with people these days. I don't have a crystal ball. I usually tell them that all we can do is make the best decisions possible today based on the information we have. We can't opt out of CPP whether we're self-employed or employed by a company, so it is what it is. But even though I have my own climate grief and anxiety, I remain hopeful that there will be a reason to pay into CPP each year, that one day, we will all benefit from that sweet inflation-protected income. If you want to learn more about CPP, see the Nitty Gritty in Chapter 1.

Back to Tania.

"Okay, so I've got tax refunds as one source of income," she said. "Even though it may be less next year because I start paying CPP in a few weeks."

"Correct."

"I've got my part-time job at the arena."

I wrote it down. "Anything else?"

She thought for a moment. "I don't think so. I don't get money from family, I don't do any more side hustles since I got the part-time job, and my money is in a chequing account, but it's just chilling there. Doing nothing."

"Right, so you have two Income Sources."

We worked out the nature of each.

The tax refunds were Random Income. She didn't ever know how much they would be or if they would even happen. Therefore, we did not include them in the Regular Income calculation.

Her part-time job, however, was reoccurring. She worked 12 hours each week for $16.75 per hour.

"How much less will I make an hour once I start having CPP come off?" she asked.

"We can use an online income tax calculator[†] to find something called your average tax rate. This will be an estimate of the CPP, EI, and income tax you may have to pay based on your income for the year. It can't be guaranteed. You'd have to confirm with your employer."

We looked up the basic personal amount for Alberta, where Tania was living. At the time, it was $15,780 for Alberta and $15,000 for Canada.

"Do you think you'll earn more than $15,000?"

"Not while I'm in school, no. I work 12 hours a week, but I usually take holidays and March break off, plus two weeks in the summer. So, I'm only working 48 weeks a year. (52 weeks – 4 weeks' vacation)."

"Let's double-check."

We did some quick math.

"If you earn $16.75 an hour and work 12 hours a week, that's $201 ($16.75 x 12 hours) per working week before tax or deductions. Which is $9,648 ($201 x 48 weeks) per year. That's under the threshold for Phase 1, so they likely won't take income tax off. But, probably not in Phase 2 when you're full-time."

I plunked $9,648 into the online income tax calculator. The average tax rate is 5.42%, which is what she will owe in CPP once she's

---

† Tax rate from https://www.wealthsimple.com/en-ca/tool/tax-calculator /alberta.

over 18, but she won't owe tax because she makes below the basic personal amount.

"This can be a bit of tricky math here for lots of people," I said.

She nodded. "I'm here for it."

I smiled. "Okay, if your average tax rate is 5.42%, then you are keeping 94.58% of your income. I got this by subtracting 5.42% from 100% (100% – 5.42%). Make sense?"

"I think I'm following. So, of all the money I get, 5.42% of it is not actually mine."

"Exactly. You keep 94.58% of the $16.75 you earn each hour."

"The deductions are CPP once I'm 18 and Employment Insurance, but not tax yet because I'm under the threshold."

"You got it." I brought back the Regular Income chart. "Now we can estimate your Predictable Income amount *after deductions*. It is $15.84 (94.58% of $16.75)."

Tania's Regular Income Calculation for Phase 1

PHASE 1 Income Source	Random	Predictable	Reoccurring	Included in Regular Income	Taxable? What rate?	A Predictable Income amount after tax $	B How many times in the next 4 weeks?	C Total Regular Income for next 4 weeks (A x B)
Tax refund	X		No	No				
Part-time job		X	X	Yes	Yes 5.42%	$15.84	48 (12 hours/ week x 4 weeks)	$760.32 ($15.84 x 48)
Full-time job								
TOTAL								$760.32

"Now we know that in the next four weeks, your total Regular Income will be $760.32," I said.

"And I can use that to estimate how much money I'll make between now and starting university."

"Yes, and we'll use this Regular Income to calculate what you think you'll earn beyond the next four months. That's called your Projected Future Income."

"My Future Income for part-time work is from now, the start of January, to when I would start full-time work in July. So, I basically have—January, February, March, April, May, June—six months of part-time income."

I nodded.

She typed into her computer. I couldn't see what, but had a feeling she was calculating in a spreadsheet.

Tania lifted her head and looked at me. "That means my Future Income for the next six months is $4,561.92 ($760.32 x 6 months)."

"That's great!" I said.

She sat back. I could see she was excited. "Can I try to figure out the Projected Future Income for Phase 2 by myself?"

"I'd love it," I said.

She shared her screen with me and I saw the Future Income Calculator I had sent her in a spreadsheet.

"Step 1," she said. "Forty hours per week." She wrote "40" in the spreadsheet.

I nodded.

"Step 2," she said. "I take home $15.84 per hour." She went to type that into the calculator, but I stopped her.

"Not the right number."

She looked up. "No?"

I shook my head. "That's the after-deductions number when you made *below* the basic income threshold and had no tax. We have to figure out what tax rate we use here. For Step 2, just use the full amount from your employment contract."

"That's $16.75 per hour for 40 hours," she said, then punched 40 x $16.75 into the calculator. "So it's $670 per week *before* deductions."

"Exactly."

"Okay, now I see. Step 3, I estimate the tax rate using the online calculator, right?"

"Yep."

"For the year?"

"For the year. Because you pay taxes on the entire year of income from January 1st to December 31st."

She hunkered over her keyboard again. "So if I work 48 weeks a year and earn $670 per week, my total estimated income before deductions for the year will be around $32,160 ($670 x 48)." This was for 2023. She looked up, excited. "Is that real?"

"Yeah!"

She scrunched up her face. "Okay, but I'll definitely owe tax."

"For sure."

She flipped her screen to another page and clicked on a personal finance blog with an income tax estimator. She put the estimated income of $32,160 into the calculator.

"It says I'll pay approximately $5,180 in deductions," she said.

"So, what's your effective tax rate?" I asked.

She looked at the screen. "It's 16.11% ($5,180/$32,160)."

"Great job. It's a bit of a messy timeline for you because you're part time for some of the year and full time for the rest. But this is a great estimate."

"Which means I keep 83.89% (100% – 16.11%) of my income." She smiled. "I can live with that!"

I smiled.

"Wait. The number here is a bit different than the estimation from

Tania's Projected Future Income Calculation for Phase 2

Income Source	Random	Predictable	Reoccurring	Included in Regular Income	Taxable? What rate?	A Predictable Income amount after tax $	B How many times in the next year?	C Total Regular Income for next year
PHASE 2								
Tax refund	X			No	No			
Part-time job								
Full-time job		X	X	Yes	16.11%	$14.05 (83.89% x $16.75)	1,920 (40 x 48)	$26,976
TOTAL								$26,976

your calculator and also from our estimated rate. Not by much, but why?"

I sighed. "These are all approximations and estimates. The goal is to get as close as possible for budgeting purposes. But it's never going to be exact. There are lots of other things at play when estimating take-home income and taxes owing. Maybe you miss a day of work because you're sick. Maybe you work overtime or don't take vacation. Maybe there are some other tax credits. Tracking and projecting income is a bit of an art."

"Got it. So I keep $14.05 of my $16.75 on average."

I leaned closer. "With this information, we can answer your first question. How much money can you count on coming in between now and the start of school in 20 months?"

She sat back for a moment, looking over the screen. Then, she leaned in again.

"I will take home $4,561.92 while I'm part-time, between now and the end of June." I watched her put that into the spreadsheet.

"Then I add $26,976, my estimated income after deductions for the year between July 1 and the end of next June. In total, I'll have $31,537.92 ($4,561.92 + $26,976)." She furrowed her brow. "What about next July and August?"

I smiled. "Want to try calculating those yourself?"

"I do." She looked at the screen. "I can estimate it by using the same Income Tracker thing."

"You can."

She filled it out, then sat back. "So, every four weeks, or approximate month, my total projected future Regular Income after deductions is $2,248 ($14.05 x 40 x 4)."

"Looks good to me," I said.

"And I just multiply that by two months. $4,496 ($2,248 x 2)."

"You got it. What's the total?"

She added them all up.

"The $4,561.92 from part-time in Phase 1, plus $26,976 from one year, plus $4,496 for the last two months before school is $36,033.92!"

"Amazing work!"

"That feels good to know." She paused. "Makes working when I'm in school feel worth it."

"How so?"

"Well, it's hard to work and go to school. My paycheques feel small because I'm part-time, so I often wonder if it's worth all the stress and effort. But knowing that the part-time work leads to the full-time work is motivating."

"That makes sense."

"Plus, when I see the part-time income as just over $4,500 of money that I get to keep, it feels way more motivating to keep working."

"Hmmm. What would make it feel unmotivating?" I asked.

She thought about it for a moment. "$4,500 is almost half my tuition. If I left my part-time job, I wouldn't have that money coming in. It's a lot of money actually. If it was only a few hundred dollars to put toward school, that wouldn't feel motivating. Like, I'm knocking myself out for money that I can only spend on lunch and not putting anything toward school. For me, that would be a non-starter."

"What I'm hearing is, when you have the full Future Income projected this way, you can see that you'll have enough money coming in over the next twenty months that you'll be able to spend a bit for day-to-day life and also save some."

"Yeah."

"And because you're able to save, it feels like there's a point to working and doing that really hard balance between work and school."

She nodded. "And when I'm at school next year, I feel like working will be financially motivating even if I can't save anything, as long as it helps keep me out of debt. Like, I'm working to not go into debt, not to save."

"That is super motivating."

"Worth the grind, as long as my grades don't suffer."

"Totally."

I was so happy for Tania. At last she knew how much money would realistically be coming to her over the next 20 months, before university. Now we could make some plans. Stay tuned for more of Tania's story in Part 2: Save Your Money.

CHAPTER 2 NITTY GRITTY

What Is a T4?

- A T4 is also called a Statement of Remuneration Paid.

- It's a document that you get from your employer when you have a job. It shows how much you earned at that place of employment for the year and how much was deducted in income taxes, CPP, and EI if applicable.

- It shows other things too. For more information, visit https://www .canada.ca/en/revenue-agency/services/tax/businesses/topics /payroll/completing-filing-information-returns/t4-information -employers/t4-slip.html.

What Is EI (Employment Insurance)?

- You likely must pay into EI with an employment job even if you are younger than 18.

- EI provides you with money if you get laid off from your job.

- How much you receive depends on how long you worked and what you earned. You can get up to 55% of your income from your job up to a certain maximum.

- For more information, visit https://www.canada.ca/en/services /benefits/ei/ei-regular-benefit.html.

Your Estimated Tax Rate

- You can estimate your taxes owing and your tax rate with an online tax calculator like this: https://www.wealthsimple.com/en-ca /tool/tax-calculator. Please note: you may find your answers differ slightly from the ones in the book. That is because the tax rates change year to year and when these numbers were calculated for the book, it was a different year than when you're reading this.

Do You Know Your Stuff?

Test your knowledge with these True or False questions.

QUESTION 1: You can estimate the amount of money that comes in after taxes by subtracting your marginal tax rate from 100%. For example, if your marginal tax rate is 20%, you keep 80% (100% − 20%).

False. Use your AVERAGE tax rate, not marginal. Tricky!

QUESTION 2: The definition of your Future Income is the money you think will come in after deductions beyond the next four weeks, usually the next year. *True.*

QUESTION 3: Anyone who works a T4 employment job has to deduct Employment Insurance (EI) automatically. *True.*

QUESTION 4: You're doing a great job. Math and money can be a topic that some people find stressful.

True! But that doesn't mean you can't do it! Everyone can take control of their finances, even if it feels like a big chore.

QUESTION 5: Anyone who works a T4 employment job has to deduct Canada Pension Plan (CPP) automatically.

False. Only those 18 years and older deduct CPP.

HOMEWORK

Calculate your Future Income.

STEP 1: Calculate your Regular Income (Chapter 1).

For example, Tania had $2,248 ($14.05 x 40 x 4) for the next four weeks (approximate month) after deductions.

STEP 2: Figure out your projecting timeline.

How far into the future do you want to project? For example, for the next six months or the next 12 months.

STEP 3: Calculate your Future Income. For example, if you are projecting six months in the future: $2,248 x 6 = $13,488. If you are projecting 12 months in the future: $2,248 x 12 = $26,976.

Meet Mia,
the Allowance Advancer

AGE:	13
SIBLING STATUS:	Middle kid between two sisters
INCOME SOURCE:	Has a regular allowance
CURRENT SAVINGS:	$0

I met Mia a few months ago. Her mom booked the appointment for her. I had met her mom, Sofia, earlier that year. She was frustrated that her middle child, Mia, blew through her allowance every week, shopping and constantly begging for more money.

"I wasn't like that, and her older sister isn't like that," Sofia said to me. "It's like the money just falls through her fingers. Should I stop giving her an allowance?"

"What does she need to pay for with the allowance?" I asked.

"She's supposed to pay for lunch and extra clothes. I take the girls shopping for winter clothes and summer clothes. Twice a year. That's it. If they want more than that, it's up to them. I'm not paying for these trendy brand-name things they like for one month and then get sick of." She waved a hand in the air, as if to push the thought away.

"I remember spending so much of my own money on a teddy bear backpack in 1996 and a Little Miss T-shirt when I was 11. I thought they would never go out of style." I rolled my eyes. "Oh, the 90s."

Sofia and I laughed together. "I remember those. But I didn't fall victim to trends then, or now," she said matter-of-factly.

"I'm jealous," I joked. "And I bet Mia is too."

Sofia sighed. "I don't know what to do with her. Should I stop giving her money until she learns to save?"

I waited a moment before responding. "Sofia, how can she learn to save if she doesn't get any money to practise with?"

She gave me a look and then smiled. "Okay. I get it." Then she paused. "But would you meet with Mia? I'll pay for the meeting and I'll bring her. Just a short meeting to give her some tips on budgeting and how to manage her allowance better so she stops running out of money each week. I won't be in the room. She needs to feel free to ask you whatever she wants."

"I'd be so happy to do this."

Three weeks later, Mia and I sat down together. Her mom was in the waiting room.

"Hey, Mia," I said, all smiles.

"Hi!" Her voice was bubbly and happy, and she was so stylish. She wore fresh white plastic clogs with charms, jeans, and a crop top, and she had long, stylized nails that sparkled. I couldn't tell if her nails were real or fake, but either way, they were awesome.

"How are you today?" I asked as we both sat down at my desk.

"Great!" she said. "I'm really excited to be here." She pulled out a beautiful blue notebook with a matching pen.

I liked Mia already.

"Okay," I started. "What would you like to get out of today?"

She looked up, and then at me. "I need to figure out why I can't seem to live off my current allowance."

"What do you mean by that?"

"Like, not live off. I don't have to pay rent or anything, but to make my allowance work for me. I'm constantly running out of money, and I can't save anything."

"What's important about being able to save your allowance?"

She gave me a confused look. "Isn't saving, like, a life skill?"

"For sure. I'm just wondering how saving up your allowance would help you."

She shrugged. "To be honest, I just want to be able to save up enough so I can afford some of the things my mom won't buy me."

"Like what?"

"A dress for grade 8 grad. My mom said that I have enough beautiful dresses and that I'm only 13, so what will be special about prom if I go all out now?" She rolled her eyes. "But she said she'd match whatever I saved for a new dress."

"Like, you save $50, she matches that, and you get $100?"

She smiled. "Exactly. Up to $100."

"How much is the dress you hope for?"

She pulled out her phone and opened up her photos to show me an amazing blue dress. It was $200. She lovingly scrolled through photos of it.

"It's beautiful," I said.

"I'm obsessed. But it's $200." She put up her hands. "I know, I know. But it's the perfect dress. And even with my mom's matching, I can't get it. I make $20 a week from allowance, but I can never save."

"Got it," I said. "Do you have any other sources of income besides your allowance?" I asked.

She shook her head. "Nope. That's it."

I filled out the Regular Income Calculation chart and showed it to her.

"You can see that your total Regular Income, or monthly income, is $80."

Mia's Regular Income Calculation

Income Source	Random	Predictable	Reoccurring	Included in Regular Income	Taxable? What rate?	A Predictable Income amount after tax $	B How many times in the next 4 weeks?	C Total Regular Income for next 4 weeks (A x B)
Allowance		X	X	Yes	0%	$20	4	$80
TOTAL								$80

She looked over the form and nodded. "Yep!"

"What would be the ideal amount of money you want to save?"

"Well, all of it. Then I could get the dress way sooner. But I can't even save $10 a week. I've tried to save as low as $5 a week, but I have to pay for stuff, and I really feel like $20 is not enough for the week."

"Hmm," I said. "That's interesting. Let's look at the weeks you tried to save money and couldn't. When was the last time you tried to put $5 aside?"

"Every week."

"What do you mean?"

"Every Friday my mom gives me $20 if I've done all the chores I need to do to earn my allowance. I have one of those kid bank accounts and app that's linked to my chores.* On Friday, if I've done all my chores, I get $20. I used to keep it in cash before, but I'd have to hide it from my sister. She's going through a stealing phase."

I raised my eyebrows. "How old is she?"

"Ten. She does it just to make me mad! I don't actually think she would spend the money."

"What happens after you've hidden the $5?"

"I usually have zero money by Monday morning for lunch.

Maybe, if I've been really good, I'll have $5 left for lunch money on Monday, but then I'm broke for the rest of the week until Friday again."

"What are you spending on over the weekend?" I asked.

"If I go to the movies with my friends, I pay for it. My mom doesn't give me more money for that. It's $15 for a movie, and that's if I sneak in my own popcorn from home. So, if I go to the movies, I'm done for the week."

"It's so expensive."

"I know! And, like, I don't have a licence, and I'm 13. The movies are, like, all we do."

"Okay, what about on a weekend when you don't go to the mov-ies?" I asked.

"If we go to the mall, I usually spend $10 on nails or some jewellery. But again, then I have $5 left for the rest of the week for lunches."

"How much is lunch?"

"My friends and I usually split lunch, but $5 is barely enough for a day. Then, I have nothing for the rest of the week, and I can't go out for lunch with my pals. Everything is so expensive."

"It really is," I said. "That's inflation* for you."

She nodded, then tilted her head. "What exactly is inflation?"

I smiled. "Inflation is the increase in the price of things over time. The cost of your life goes up over time."

She looked a bit confused.

"For example, when I was your age, I also spent my allowance or part-time job money on movies, clothes, and lunch at the school caf-eteria, but the movie was $5, lunch was $2, and a shirt was $10."

"Oh my God, I could definitely save if life was that cheap."

"Yeah, but my allowance was only $15 a week."

"Oh," she said.

"Exactly. So, if I wanted to buy a shirt, it was almost my whole week's allowance. Or I only had enough for lunch money every day and no movies."

"At least the movies weren't your entire weekly allowance."

"For sure."

"And food is so expensive. I need $10 for lunch, not $5. I'm not even buying expensive salads, I'm buying muffins and a tea, or a sandwich. My mom doesn't understand. She gave my sister $20 a week six years ago and still thinks that's enough because it was enough for her. But it's not enough. I need a raise."

I thought about this for a moment. Sofia had really made it seem like Mia was spending out of control, but, when I looked at the breakdown of her money, it really was tight with the cost of movies and food and how much those have gone up.

"Mia," I said, "I actually don't think you're wrong."

Her eyes opened wide. "What? You think I should ask my mom for a raise?"

I could tell she was shocked.

"Not from a place of greed, but I do think the cost of living has gone up significantly in the last six years. Your mom is basing the amount on what worked for your sister, but because of inflation, that $20 isn't going as far as it used to and you're struggling."

"Yes!" she said, almost relieved. "Yes. I mean, I definitely spend money, but so did my sister. But things were cheaper then."

"How much more do you think you'd need per week?"

She thought about this. "Honestly, I'd love $30, but I think my mom would pass out if I asked her. But if I had an extra $5 a week, I could save that $5 and use the full $20 for life."

"Have you ever asked before?"

"No!" she said. "I know she's just going to say I spend too much."

"Do you think your mom can afford the extra $5? If not, then you want to tread lightly there."

"I definitely think she can, I think she just sees me as this big spender."

Since Sofia's mom was a client, I knew the financial landscape of the family. I knew Sofia could afford the extra $5 a week without harming her finances. I also knew Sofia wanted Mia to learn the value of money. I thought that maybe an inflationary raise would help give Mia the opportunity to save and spend at the same time so she could build the habit of saving.

"Maybe I can help make a case here for you. You're basically negotiating a salary increase. This is a life skill that you can take with you one day into a job."

"Exciting," Mia said.

I grabbed a piece of paper and wrote, *"Asking for a Raise."*

"Let's pretend that your chores are your job and your mom is your employer."

She grinned. "I like it."

I wrote, "Step 1: Can the employer afford it?"

"The first thing you want to do is ensure the company you work for, a.k.a. your mom, can actually afford to give you a raise. In a job, if you work for a company that is having a hard economic time, asking for a raise can be fruitless because the company may not have the money to give it to you."

I put a check mark beside Step 1. "We think this is a yes. Let's run with that for the time being."

She nodded and I wrote, *"Step 2: Your raise makes sense compared to peers."*

"The second thing to do when asking for a raise is to establish that you're due for one given the economic climate."

Mia furrowed her brow. "What does that mean?"

I thought for a moment. "It's a way of asking if the amount you're hoping for makes sense, given what other parents who are similar to your family pay their kids and what's going on in the world."

"Right. Well, my pals all get $25 to $30 a week."

"So, if this were a job at a company, and we know that the company can afford to give raises, I'd say your salary is lower than your peers or colleagues who are doing the same work as you."

"Yes. That's fair to say."

"And, in the greater economy, inflation really has made life more expensive." I opened up a link on my computer. "See this?" I showed her an inflation calculator from the World Data website.[†]

"If you put $20 in the Original Amount box, then put 2018—six years ago—in the Start Year box and 2024 in the End Year box, you can see that $20 is actually only worth $16.34 today."

"Do you mean that's what inflation did to my money?"

"Yes. If you show this to your mom, you can show her that $20 has lost its value."

"I'm loving this."

I beamed. "I think you've got a good argument for a raise here. Lastly, we have Step 3: Show your value." I showed her the page. "You need to show you're worth it."

"Like, the chores?"

"Exactly. In the workplace, when you grow up, if you're not doing a good job, then it doesn't matter if the company can afford it, or that your peers are paid more, or that there's a good economic argument for a raise. If you're not doing a good job, you probably won't get a raise."

"That makes sense," she agreed. "How do I show the value of my chores to my mom?"

"What are the chores you do right now for your current allowance?" I asked.

---

† https://www.worlddata.info/america/canada/inflation-rates.php

She listed them off. "Vacuum the entire apartment once a week. Take out the garbage and recycling, and clean the bathroom once a week."

"That's great!"

"Is it?" She laughed. "I also have to clean my room each morning before school and help with dishes, but I'm not paid for those. My mom says that's just what you do to be part of the household."

I nodded. "Does she track your chores?"

Mia shook her head. "No."

"Well, tracking is a great way for you to show that you're actually doing the work you said you were going to do!"

I opened up another spreadsheet and made a weekly checklist template with each chore.

"You can print this off and show her each week."

"I get that, but how can I convince her to give me $25 a week?"

"What do you think the benefit is to your mom when you vacuum, do the garbage, and clean the bathroom?"

She thought for a moment. "Time saved? My little sister can't do the hard-core cleaning yet, and my older sister moved out for university. If I didn't do it, she'd have to, or else she'd have to hire a cleaning service."

"Agreed," I said. "So, time-wise, what's cheaper for your mom, $5 a week, or $150 for cleaning service once a month?"

"Definitely $5 a week."

"Do you do a good job?"

She nodded. "I actually do."

"Then you're a steal! You can show your mom how much time and money you are saving her when you ask for the raise."

"Thank you. This helps me ask her without feeling guilty about it, like I'm some sort of greedy, ungrateful kid."

"I'm glad."

"The inflation stuff helps a lot too. I'm not imagining things. The $20 is not the same as what my sister got."

"And I wonder if $25 will be the same when your younger sister starts her allowance."

"Huh," she said. "I didn't even think of that."

"How do you feel about everything? Did you get what you came for?"

She nodded, then hesitated.

"What's up?" I asked.

She smiled, sheepishly. "The dress."

"Yes."

"Let's say I ask for my raise and my mom actually says yes, and I save the $5 a week and spend the $20. That's almost five months for me to save the $100 ($100/$5 = 20 weeks) for the dress. That's forever!"

"The art of waiting," I joked.

"For real, though, that's so long. It will be over by then. Grad is in four months."

"Well, you could try for some bonus money."

"Like, bonus chores for money?"

"Exactly. Big tasks that really save your mom money or time. What are some of the chores your mom does that she can't stand, or that she hires out, that you could do instead?"

She thought for a moment, then sat up with a "eureka" expression. "Oh! I know!"

"What, what?!" I asked, excited.

"Grocery shopping."

"Ugh. I hate grocery shopping too."

"Oh my God, my mom hates it. She's so busy with work, which means it's always got to be on a weeknight when she's exhausted or on the weekend when she wants to enjoy her time."

"Taking care of the shopping would definitely save her valuable time."

"Definitely."

"How much do you think that's worth?"

"Well, a few times we've ended up ordering takeout, which is expensive, or using those grocery delivery companies, also expensive, because she didn't shop. But if I shopped, we'd have groceries."

"Sounds like you'd be saving time and money. That's a big deal and hugely motivating for someone to say yes if they can afford to."

"I'm sure she'd rather pay me every now and then than a fast food or a delivery business."

"I bet."

"So, what if I ask for something huge. Like, $10 for a grocery shop. Less than takeout for the three of us. Even more so if my sister is home."

"I think it sounds like it makes sense."

"And I don't have to do it all the time. But, if I did it twice a month, that's enough for my dress."

"Your mom may only want to do this every now and then, but I definitely think it's a great bonus chore to bring up in your salary ne-

Mia's Projected Future Income Calculation

Income Source	Random	Predictable	Reoccurring	Included in Regular Income	Taxable? What rate?	A. Predictable Income amount after tax $	B. How many times in the next 4 weeks?	C. Total Future Income for next 4 weeks (A x B)
Allowance	X	X	Yes	0%	$25	4	$100
Bonus chore	X	X	Yes	0%	$10	2	$20
TOTAL							$120

gotiation. Let's look at your Future Income with your potential raise and two bonus chores each month."

"That's $120 this month!" I said.

"Wow. That feels like so much money!" she said.

"If it works out, you will have earned it."

"I hope my mom agrees."

"Me too. But you have to be okay with it if she doesn't. It's her money and her call. However, I think you have a very convincing argument, and I really do think it will save her time and money."

"This is definitely not where I expected this meeting to go."

"I'm curious. What did you think I was going to say?"

"That I'm terrible with money."

"You're 13! You are too young to be terrible with money. It's just a skill set you haven't had a chance to practise yet, and life is expensive. When life is expensive, one of the first things you can do is see if there's another way to bring in more money or diversify your income stream. Let's try that first before we start reducing all your expenses."

"I like that idea. That I can earn my way out of this instead of cutting, cutting, cutting. And it doesn't have to be a big amount. Just $5 a week and a bonus chore. It makes it feel doable."

"It's often the same with adults. Sometimes earning just a bit more can make all the difference. It doesn't have to be a million dollars, y'know?"

"Totally," she said thoughtfully. "But, I definitely want to touch a mil' one day."

I looked at her, sort of confused. "Touch a mil'?" I asked, and then it came to me. "Do you mean earn a million dollars?"

She grinned. "Yes."

I burst out laughing. "Got it."

I'm so old.

CHAPTER 3 NITTY GRITTY

What Is Inflation?

- Inflation is the rising costs of goods and services over time.

- You can read more on the Bank of Canada website here: https://www.bankofcanada.ca/core-functions/monetary-policy/inflation/.

- To see interactive charts showing how inflation impacts prices over time, look here: https://www.statcan.gc.ca/en/subjects-start/prices_and_price_indexes/consumer_price_indexes.

Youth Chequing Accounts

- There are many types of youth bank accounts in Canada. Almost every bank has one. Be sure to check out the options and do your research!

- Look for accounts that don't have fees.

- Look for accounts that will help to track your spending.

- Some accounts have reward programs.

- Look for accounts will allow you to pay for things with tap technology (but be careful with how easy it is to overspend).

- Some accounts allow parent monitoring.

- Some chequing accounts are linked to an app that track chores (eg. https://www.mydoh.ca/).

Do You Know Your Stuff?

Test your knowledge with these True or False questions.

QUESTION 1: Your allowance is not taxable. *True.*

QUESTION 2: Allowance should NOT be included in your Regular Income calculations.

False. It is predictable and reoccurring.

QUESTION 3: "Touch a mil'" means make a million dollars one day.

True.

QUESTION 4: Inflation makes the cost of living go up over time.

True.

QUESTION 5: When asking for a raise, the first step is to show your employer that you can save them time or money.

False. Here are the three steps to asking for a raise:

STEP 1: Ensure that your employer can afford to pay more.

STEP 2: Prove that a raise makes sense given what other people who are doing the same things as you are paid and given what's happening in the world.

STEP 3: Show how you save your employer time or money.

Meet Oliver, the Kid Who Seems to Have It All

AGE:	16
SIBLING STATUS:	Only child
INCOME SOURCE:	Not allowed to have a job because he needs to keep his grades up; doesn't need an allowance because he can "get money from my parents whenever I ask"
CURRENT SAVINGS:	$500 in an online chequing account; an RESP (Registered Education Savings Plan)* for university (if he gets in); a stock simulator account with $5,000 in it—Oliver makes stock trades to practise, then his dad executes the trades for real in an online investment account that Oliver will have access to when he's 18 (the age of majority in Ontario)

I originally met Oliver in an interview for this book. Looking at Oliver on paper, you may be thinking that he has it all, right?

Don't be so quick to judge. One of the biggest lessons I've learned over my time in this field is to never make assumptions about someone's financial life based on what you *think* they have. On paper, Oliver has a lot. But having money can sometimes come with its own unique set of problems.

"I've got about $500 in my chequing account," he said. I hadn't asked how much was in his chequing account, but he offered up this information.

"That's a lot for someone your age!" I said cheerily.

He shrugged. "I guess."

It felt like he wanted me to know that he didn't think $500 was a lot of money. "And how do you earn your money?" I was taking notes.

He thought a moment, moving a basketball back and forth between his hands, then he said, "Different places. I don't have an income, like a job or an allowance. So, birthday money. Holiday money. Random money that my dad will put in there when I ask."

I nodded. "Is that your spending money then?"

He shrugged. "Sort of."

"What do you mean, sort of?" I was curious.

He shifted back and forth, but then finally answered. "Yeah, it's my spending money."

The fact that it took him so long to confirm that it was his spending money seemed strange to me. Most of the teenagers I had interviewed were definitely aware of their spending money.

I smiled. "Yet you don't seem convinced that it is your spending money."

He shrugged. "It's supposed to be."

"Supposed to be what?"

"My spending money. It's where all my money goes when I get it. Like, my income. Then I take money from there when I need it."

"That's interesting," I said.

"What is?"

"You refer to it as your income, but you just said that you don't have an income."

"I guess I do," he corrected. "Gifts, birthday money, that kind of thing." He looked at me expectantly.

"Gotcha."

Hmmm. Do I go into it? Yes, I do.

"Technically, you don't have something I call a Regular Income, Oliver. You've got money, but you don't have an income."

Oliver looked confused. "What's the difference?"

"As far as financial planning goes, your Regular Income is the money you have coming in, after any tax deductions, in the next four weeks. It's predictable or reoccurring, or both."

"So, because mine are all big gifts, they don't count?"

"In a sense, yes. It's not that they don't count—as in, they aren't important—but they are random. You can't necessarily predict them. Sure, you know you'll probably get money on your birthday, but you don't really know how much or exactly when it will come. So you can't count on it when you're trying to figure out how much money you can spend for budgeting purposes."

He nodded. "Okay, I get that. Like, because it's random, it's hard to figure out what I'm able to spend every week or month."

"Exactly. Your type of money is the hardest to track for everyone. Adults, young people. Everyone with Random Income," I said.

"Really?"

"Yes. Because it's all random. If you were a financial planning client, it would be hard for me to include your income in my tracking system as Regular Income to make a budget, and it would also be hard to predict your Future Income for saving up."

He seemed disappointed, or irritated.

He set the basketball on the floor. "Maybe some of it isn't random. Let me pull up my app," he said. "And see the money that's come in over the last four weeks."

I was surprised he didn't know what money had come into his bank account over the last four weeks. Most of the youth I'd met or have worked with had some idea. He tried logging in but forgot his password. He had to wait to reset it.

"It's been a minute," he said without looking up from his phone. "Sorry."

"No prob."

Once he pulled up the account, he gave his phone to me to see the transactions. In the last month, there hadn't been any, in or out, besides a bank fee and one transaction at a sporting goods store for $150 three weeks earlier.

I handed back the phone and looked at him. "Okay, next question. What do you like to spend money on?"

"Normal stuff. Movies, clothes, lunch."

"How do you buy lunch?"

"What do you mean?" he asked, almost bashful.

"Well, I'm just curious because you have $500 in that account and no transactions for a month besides a sporting goods store. Do you pack a lunch every day? Or have a cash allowance?"

"I told you, I'm not allowed to get an allowance because my dad gives me money when I ask for it."

"Oh, okay," I said. "So when you want to go out for lunch or something, your folks cover it." I was nodding and dutifully taking notes.

"Not really."

I stopped writing. "Sorry, Oliver, I'm a bit confused," I said.

"My dad thinks spending money on lunch is dumb. A waste when I could take my lunch. So most times I have to borrow money off one of my buddies."

I was confused. "So, this $500 is more like savings, not your spending money."

"It's supposed to be my spending money."

My face scrunched up. "But you don't spend it?"

"Well, I . . ." He trailed off.

"It's alright," I said. "You don't have to tell me."

He squirmed and looked away. "It's okay. In theory, it's my spending money, but I'm not actually allowed to spend it."

Now we were getting somewhere. "Tell me about that."

He let out a big sigh. "My dad monitors the account."

"I've seen that a lot, especially with youth accounts."

"Yeah, but he's a drill sergeant about it."

"What do you mean?"

He leaned in, like he was afraid his pals in the hallway could hear us. "When I actually spend any money from that account, he's all over me. About what I did. Why I did it and how I need to be responsible and saving and learn the value of a dollar and not be wasteful."

"I see."

He got louder. "So, like, I can never *actually* spend it. Any of it! On anything. It's supposed to be 'there for me to spend,' but it's so messed up because I don't even have the debit card. He keeps it! I'm not even allowed to carry it. I have to ask to use it every time and explain what I'm about to spend money on." He was exasperated. "But I'm also not allowed to get a job or have an allowance. I have to endlessly ask for money, then I get shamed for using it."

Whoa. I did not see that coming. I felt for him but didn't say anything right away.

He sat back and looked up at the ceiling with his hands on his forehead. "Ugh, I know what you're thinking."

"Yeah?" I raised an eyebrow. "What am I thinking?"

He let out a short laugh, then lowered his hands and head and looked at me. "Poor little rich kid, right?"

"Hmm," I said, after a long pause. "No. That's not what I'm thinking." At this point, I genuinely didn't know that Oliver's family was wealthy.

"Sure it is. I know that's what my friends think too."

"Have they said that to you?"

"Yeah, some of them. A couple times."

"That doesn't feel very kind."

"It's because I have to borrow money off them sometimes to pay for things that my dad disapproves of. Like lunch out or coffee. But they know I have parents who randomly give me money because sometimes my dad will just give me $100."

"That's tough."

He scoffed.

"Oliver, I'm serious. That's actually really tough. It sucks," I said.

His shoulders sank in. It was the first time I felt like his defences were down. "It does."

I paused for a moment, not sure what to do next. Then I blurted out, "I want to help. There's lots of really great strategies—"

"No, no, it's fine." He shook his head. "I'm totally fine. Ignore me." He put his hands up, as if to push away the idea of help. "Honestly, I should be more grateful. I know I am really, really lucky. Lots of people don't have money at all and here I am complaining."

I felt the window closing.

"My dad is just trying to teach me good money values. He didn't get to where he is today by blowing money on stupid things and going out for lunch every day, you know?"

Definitely a well-rehearsed speech.

We sat for a moment.

"Maybe," I said. "Maybe we just finish the interview for today, and if you want any strategies on how to navigate your personal finances, you can reach out and let me know."

"Sure." He smiled. "Then I'll know exactly how much of my money I *can't* spend each month."

I smiled with him. "Knowledge is power."

We finished the interview. He was just about to leave and turned in the doorway.

"Hypothetically, if someone under 18 wanted to hire you for . . ." He paused. "Financial coaching or strategies, could they do that?"

"Hypothetically?" I asked.

"Hypothetically," he confirmed.

"Hypothetically, yes. A minor could sign a contract as long as it's for their benefit, such as financial planning."

He nodded.

"And hypothetically, would you be willing to teach a person under 18 about personal finance strategies if they have money but not really?"

"Hypothetically, I'd be happy to." I smiled.

He raised an eyebrow. "For real?"

"For real."

We set it up. A series of short financial sessions, and Oliver was now officially a client. How exciting!

The next time we met, it was in my office. Oliver came in with his basketball and backpack. He flopped down onto the chair across from me.

"Ready?" I said.

"Yeah, I guess," he said in a nonchalant way.

Okay, he's nervous, I thought. I started out cheery. "For today, we can start by figuring out how to project your Future Income, even if your only Income Source is gifts and random money. Does that sound good?" I asked.

He nodded. I wasn't sure if he was convinced that booking these sessions was a good choice.

I pulled out the Regular Income chart. "I filled out your Regular Income chart based on the information from the interview. See? It's tough to track your income since we don't really know what's coming in or when. Could be a bunch from your parents tomorrow or nothing for several months." I showed him the chart. "Has anything changed since then?"

"Nope," he said without looking at it.

"The trick with your type of money, all random, is that you have to project out for the whole year, and then divide by 12 to get a monthly projection or by 52 if you want a weekly projection. Sort of a best guess."

"Got it," he said.

Oliver's Regular Income Calculation

Income Source	Random	Predictable	Reoccurring	Included in Regular Income	Taxable? What rate?	A — Predictable Income amount after tax $	B — How many times in the next 4 weeks?	C — Total Regular Income for next 4 weeks (A x B)
Birthday money	X			No	0%	$0		$0
Holiday money	X			No	0%	$0		$0
Asking parents for cash	X			No	0%	$0		$0
TOTAL								$0

"Let's start with Step 1. Let's guess how much money per year is coming in from each random source, starting with the most predictable. I imagine that's birthday money, yeah?"

He nodded.

"When's your birthday?" I asked.

"June 15."

Gemini. Noted.

"Sitting here in February, we know that five months from now you are likely to get money."

He nodded and looked away. "I always get something from my grandparents."

"Alright, what's the lowest amount of money you would realistically get?"

He squirmed. "Like, the least amount?"

"Yes. You want to be conservative with your estimates, but not so conservative that you're being unrealistic."

He was so uncomfortable. "This makes me feel so weird."

"Don't be silly. Tell me. How much on average, or minimum. Per birthday."

He cringed and shut his eyes. "Probably $300."

"This is hard for you to talk about, eh?"

"I just feel so uncomfortable. I'm, like, embarrassed."

"Listen, if I had a golden ticket, I'd cash it too. You don't need to feel embarrassed."

I paused for a moment. "Money is just a tool in your life tool kit. It doesn't define your worth now, 10 months from now, or 10 years from now. You've got access to more tools in your kit earlier than most, yes. But it doesn't mean you will forever. You still need to learn good financial habits so you can kick off your life with a good money relationship. Right now, you have money but no opportunity to practise the skills you'll actually need for real life."

"I guess borrowing money from pals and avoiding my dad isn't really an ideal way to learn good financial skills."

We laughed.

"It's not great," I joked.

"Okay, fine," he said and gave his head a shake. "Let's keep going."

"Wonderful. Let's talk about holiday money. How much do you usually get each year by the end of the year?"

"This is harder. Could be much more but I'm never exactly sure. I'd say $500-ish?"

"Great." I wrote it down.

"What about asking your parents for money, on an ongoing basis?" I asked carefully.

"My dad. Not my mom."

"Oh?"

"Yeah, my dad runs all my money. My mom always says, 'That's your dad's department,' any time I try to talk to her about it."

"I'm gonna put a pin in that for now."

"It's for the best. They are so old school."

"How often do you ask your dad for money?"

He thought about this for a moment. "I really try not to. But when I want to buy something like sneakers or clothes, I usually give him a heads-up that I'm going to use the money in the bank account, and then he will say, 'No, no, that's for saving, I'll pay for it.' And then he gives me the cash."

"What about the day-to-day stuff, lunch, movies, et cetera."

He shook his head. "That's the issue. It's like he's fine to give me lots of money when there's something big that he approves of, but the day-to-day stuff is tough. He says that I don't need a job or an allowance because I just have to ask him for money, but if I do ask, it's the whole shame-and-blame conversation about useless purchases, and he won't give me money. Then, if I spend money from the account anyway, I get in trouble for being irresponsible. He sees it as sneaking around because I didn't ask."

"What a cycle," I said.

"It's not great."

"Well, what's the least amount of money, per year, that you think you'd get from your dad, if you asked and it was an approved transaction?"

He thought about this. "Per year? At least $400. For sneakers, clothes, video games. Probably more, but it all depends on what I need or what he thinks I need."

I wrote it down in the chart.

"So your total annual Projected Future Income over the next 52 weeks is $1,200. Based on these estimates."

"Yeah, that makes sense."

"The next step is to divide that by 12 months and get your, sort of, monthly income."

Oliver's Future Income Calculation

Income Source	Random	Predictable	Reoccurring	Included in Regular Income	Taxable? What rate?	A Predictable Income amount after tax $	B How many times in the next 52 weeks?	C Total Future Income for next 52 weeks (A x B)
Birthday money	X				No	0%	$300	1	$300
Holiday money	X				No	0%	$500	1	$500
Asking parents for cash	X				No	0%	$200	2	$400
TOTAL								$1,200

"It's $100 a month ($1,200/12 months)," he said.

"Good head math!"

He raised an eyebrow and smiled. "That wasn't a hard one."

"Technically, you could spend about $100 a month based on your Future Income projection. If you were to do that, let's just say you did, you would eat into your current savings until June, when you get the $300 from your birthday."

I wrote it down: $500/$100 = 5 months.

"You have five months in the account already. That's actually quite perfect."

"Yeah, but I can't use the $100 a month. That would be so amazing if I could. It's like $25 a week. Perfect for movies, lunch, that kind of thing."

I thought for a moment. "Does any of your money come in cold, hard cash?"

He squinted his eyes at me. "Do you mean money my dad doesn't know about?"

I shrugged. "No, I'm asking if there's any personal money for you to manage on your own."

He smiled. "Nope."

"Well, we know that your projected income is $1,200 a year, or $100 a month on average. Maybe you can chat it out with your parents and try over the next month to live within and spend within that $25 a week so you can show them that you know how to budget, and we can follow up at the next session and see how it went?"

He nodded and let out a long breath. "I'll definitely try."

"Awesome. Maybe, with a plan, your parents will be more likely to say yes to spending it because they won't be afraid of it being overspent."

"Yeah, I could see that." He nodded. "My dad would like that I had a plan."

"Good luck!" I said as he left the office. I was nervous for him and could not wait to catch up at our second session to see how it went. My fingers were crossed for him.

CHAPTER 4 NITTY GRITTY

What Is the RESP (Registered Education Savings Plan)?

- The RESP is an account where a subscriber (usually a parent, grandparent, or family member) saves money for a child to help pay for post-secondary schooling.

- You can read more about how much goes in and what can come out here: https://www.canada.ca/en/revenue-agency/services/tax/individuals/topics/registered-education-savings-plans-resps.html.

Do You Know Your Stuff?

Test your knowledge with these True or False questions.

QUESTION 1: Gifts from family and friends are not taxable.

True.

QUESTION 2: Money can't buy happiness. *True.*

QUESTION 3: This book is awesome. *True!*

QUESTION 4: If your main income is gifts only, you can project your Regular Income by adding the amounts you think you'll get in a year and dividing by 12.

False. You do this calculation to project your Future Income. With random gifts, you can't calculate your Regular Income because there isn't one.

QUESTION 5: If a friend gives you money, this is an example of Regular Income.

False. It would be random and considered a gift.

HOMEWORK

Calculate your Future Income from gifts.

STEP 1: List all the gifts that come to you in any given year. Think holidays, birthdays, etc.

STEP 2: Calculate how much that you expect in the next 12 months from gifts only. Do not add any other income here.

STEP 3: Divide by 12 to get your Projected Future Income from gifts.

PART 2
Save Your Money

What Money Skill Do You Need to Learn Next?

The second skill you'll need to set yourself up for financial success in life is the ability to save your money. Everyone knows that saving money is a good thing, but if it were easy, everyone would do it, and no one would ever have financial issues. Truth be told, saving is hard. But with some tools in your kit, it is definitely not impossible.

Saving involves two things. The first is setting the goal and calculating how much money you need to save to get there. That's the easy part. The second part is putting that money away and not spending it. That's the hard part, and the reason so many people give up. But I promise, there are ways to keep your eyes on the goal and keep that money where you need it.

Why Is Saving Your Money an Important Skill?

Every goal you have probably comes with a price attached. Post-secondary school? That costs money. An expensive pair of shoes? Also costs money. Travel? Buying a car one day? Lots and lots of money.

Your goals and your dreams likely come with a cost, so you need to learn how to set those goals properly and save in a way that makes it possible to live your life while also achieving your goals and your dreams.

How Will You Use This Skill in the Future?

Big reveal: saving money is still one of the hardest skills for adults!

It's the entire reason I have a job! Helping people set savings goals and keep them is what I do. Setting the goal is one thing (which you will learn below). Keeping the goal is the other. If you can manage to learn that skill now, while you're young, you'll be able to repeat it when you're older and have an adult income. Being able to save is the key to reaching your dreams and feeling financially secure so you don't have to worry. And it all starts here!

What You Will Learn Throughout Part 2

- The difference between short-term savings and long-term savings

- How to set targeted savings timelines

- How to calculate how much you need to save and how long it will take you to save it

- Where to store your savings: what type of bank account or storage system to use

Buckle up! The ride starts here.

Short-Term Savings Versus Long-Term Savings

I often hear people say they need to save for a vacation, a shirt, the holidays.

I also hear things like "I need to save to go to school," or "buy a house," or "retire."

Sure, in all those scenarios, you're saving money, but what you're saving for is way different. The act of saving means that you're not spending all your money. Some is being stored somewhere else, not to be spent on day-to-day items.

Saving money means putting money aside in order to benefit or improve your financial future. This is also called improving your net worth.

The technical definition of net worth is "the total wealth of a person." But I don't like that definition because I think we can be wealthy in many aspects of our life, not just financially. You can be wealthy in friendship, health, or community. I like to think of your net worth specific to finances as "everything you have saved minus everything you owe."

For example, if you have $50 in your sock drawer but you owe your sibling $10, your net worth is $40 ($50 – $10). Just because you have $50 doesn't mean it's all yours because you owe money to someone else.

The adult version of this could be a house. You may hear a lot about houses being worth millions of dollars. In much of Canada, this is true, which is bananas . . . but that's a different book.

If a person's house is worth $1,000,000 but they have a mortgage on it for $600,000, they would have $400,000 ($1,000,000 – $600,000) in their pocket if they sold it. Which means their net worth is $400,000.

Your net worth is the major difference between short-term savings and long-term savings.

Short-term savings is money you've put aside to spend later on something big. A great example of this is saving up to buy an expensive pair of shoes. Imagine that you put aside $20 a week for 10 weeks. You'd have $200. But that money is going to be spent on shoes, so it's not improving your financial future. It's glorified spending money. Short-term savings is not real savings.

Other examples of short-term savings are putting money aside for a trip, saving for a game console, or keeping money for holiday shopping.

Long-term savings is money you've put aside that will benefit your financial future. This is money that you will use to go to post-secondary school, maybe buy a house one day, retire one day, or pay down debt (hopefully you don't have much debt in your life after reading this book).

In Part 2 of this book, you'll learn how to set short-term goals and long-term goals, and understand where to store your savings!

5

David, Who Just Couldn't Wait

AGE:	14
SIBLING STATUS:	Has a younger brother
INCOME SOURCE(S):	Old enough to legally work but hasn't found a job; random jobs in the neighbourhood
CURRENT SAVINGS:	$20 in sock drawer (on the left-hand side)

It had been a week since our first porch session, and I was excited to see David for our second.

"Hey!" David said as he walked into the porch.

"Hi, David!" I said and waved to his proud mom, who was dropping him off.

In our second session, we were going to make a plan for him to start saving some money. We sat down, and I opened up the notes I took the last time we chatted.

"Last time we figured out that you had $260 coming in over the next four weeks."

"Yes, I've collected $40 of it from the past week—$25 from tutoring and $15 from walking Luna. The rest will come in on those big babysitting weeks and with the week I'm walking Max too."

"Right! And do you still have all $40 of it?"

"Um, no," he said. "I had to buy lunch twice last week, so I only have $30 left. But I still have the $20 in my sock drawer."

I smiled. "Awesome!" I leaned back in my chair. "So, tell me, what do you want to get out of our session today?"

"I want to get a console in the next two months," he said.

"Like, a video game console?" I asked.

"Uh, yeah."

I smiled. I knew I had just aged myself.

"How much is it?"

"It's $500."

My eyes sort of bulged out of my head.

"That's a lot of money in a short time," I said. "Why give yourself a two-month timeline?"

"Because I want the console while it's still summer break. My mom is hard-core about video game time during the school year. My friends and I are all off this summer, and I want to be able to game with them for at least the month of August before school starts. It's the beginning of June now. I have Max money and tutoring money coming in this month. I think I can do it. I've already got $50."

Even though my gut said this was unrealistic, I didn't want to squash his enthusiasm. He seemed like he really believed it could work.

"Let's math it out," I said instead and picked up a pen. "When you're setting a savings goal, Step 1 is to figure out how much income is coming in over your savings targeted timeline."

"What's my savings targeted timeline? Isn't that the rest of the $260 that's coming in?"

"Well, you want to achieve your goal by August 1st. So in your case, your targeted timeline is the rest of June and all of July. We know you can count on your Regular Income for June, but what about July? We need to calculate the income you will have beyond what we know for sure in June."

"Do we do that the same way we calculated my income before?"

"Pretty much. The only difference is that we may have to guess or estimate a bit for the Future Income that's not absolutely guaranteed."

Together, we filled out David's Projected Future Income chart for the timeline he had set to reach his goal. In this case, it was the next two months, the rest of June and all of July. We knew he could count on $220 for the rest of June. That figure was $260 guaranteed less the $40 he already collected.

We also knew that babysitting Olivia would continue as he already had a July date booked. Another $60.

But tutoring stopped in July. Bummer.

Dog-walking Luna would continue three times a week for all four weeks of July, giving him a total of $60 (12 x $5).

These were all known sources of income.

"What about babysitting Sammy? Do you think you'll have a booking in July?"

He nodded. "Yes, probably at least once in July. I'll reach out today and ask if they need a night out. That would be four hours. $60."

"What about lawn mowing?"

"I think I can canvass the neighbourhood door to door. Lots of people go on vacation in July. I should probably be able to cut one a week while people are away. Or maybe I can also add watering their gardens. Yes. If I add in watering their gardens, I can probably do two, maybe even three a week in July."

"Wow. So that'd be 12 lawns or gardens at $10 each in July. $120!"

"Yeah, I'm going to make that a goal. I think watering the gardens will be a big seller."

"What about walking Max?"

"No idea. Probably not."

"So, your total Projected Future Income over your savings timeline is . . ." I tallied it up. "$300!"

David's Projected Future Income Calculation

Income Source	Random	Predictable	Reoccurring	Included in Regular Income	Tax rate*	A Predictable Income amount $	B How many times in the next 4 weeks?	C Total Regular Income
Babysitting Olivia		X	Yes		No	$60/month ($15 x 4 hours)	1	$60 ($60 x 1)
Tutoring		X	Yes		No	$25/week	0	$0
Dog-walking Luna		X	Yes		No	$5/walk	12 (3 times per week)	$60 ($5 x 12)
Babysitting Sammy	X		Yes		No	$15/hour	4	$60 ($15 x 4)
Shovelling/lawn mowing	X		Yes		No	$10/house	12	$120 ($10 x 12)
Dog-walking Max	X		Yes		No	$10/walk	0	$0 ($10 x 0)
TOTAL								$300

*Tax rate from https://www.wealthsimple.com/en-ca/tool/tax-calculator/ontario.

He was pumped.

"That's great. I can absolutely save up the $500." He was so happy. I wanted to be as happy, but I was worried.

"I'm so excited that you're excited," I started. "But I have a potentially icky reminder."

He grimaced. "What?"

"Putting aside money that you need to spend for your daily life between now and the end of your savings targeted timeline. It's money you can't save because you'll still have expenses between now and August 1st. Like, lunch for the rest of school, going to the movies in July with your pals, and all that other life stuff."

"Shoot. You're right."

"I hate when that happens."

David laughed. "Okay, I usually live off of Olivia babysitting and Luna money each month, but have no spending after that. I save all of it."

I looked at the projecting tool. "If you use up the money you make babysitting Olivia and walking Luna, then your normal expenses have to be $120 ($60 + $60) each month."

He nodded.

"That's approximately $30 a week ($120 per month/4 weeks)."

He nodded again.

"How many weeks between now and August 1st?"

He looked at his phone calendar. "Seven."

"So, how much do you need to set aside for real-life spending?" I asked.

He grabbed my calculator and calculated $30 x 7 weeks. "I need $210."

"Now, calculate how much money you will have left for the console after you put aside $210 for daily life."

Calculator out again.

"I have my $20 in savings," he said.

"Yep."

"Plus $30 I still have from working this past week."

"Yep."

"$220 expected in June."

"Yep."

"$300 expected in July."

"Exactly."

"That's $570."

"Less . . . ?"

"Less $210 for daily life leaves $360."

"Precisely."

He slumped back in the chair. "So, I'll have a shortfall of $140 ($500 – $360)."

I nodded. "That's Step 3. Calculate the shortfall—if there is one."

He looked disappointed.

"Can you wait one or two more months?" I suggested. "Maybe September or October wouldn't be that bad?"

He shook his head. "I really want to be able to play this summer."

"Well, there are three ways to reach your savings goals. First, earn more. Second, spend less. Third, extend your timeline."

"Maybe a combination of the first two?" he said.

"What do you think is realistic?"

He thought for a moment. "What if I only spend $20 a week, not $30. That would only be $140 ($20 x 7 weeks) for spending money in the next seven weeks."

I nodded. "Do you think you can live within $20 a week?"

"For sure," he said, very confidently.

"And what about earning more?"

"If I reduce my spending to $140 from $210, I save an extra $70 ($210 – $140). So my $140 shortfall will only be $70 ($140 – $70). I think I can earn that."

"Maybe tutoring for summer school could work," I said. "Or a week or two of dog-sitting?"

"Yeah, or maybe I babysit more. I'll figure it out."

He totally skimmed over details with me. I call this "Racing to Yes."

To be honest, I didn't feel like his plan was realistic. Reducing his spending by $10 a week was a 33% decrease ($10/$30), and that's a big deal! Also, his plan to suddenly earn an extra $70, which he hadn't felt he could do earlier, also felt rushed and unreliable.

I sighed. "David, I'm worried this is a bit unrealistic."

He grinned wide. "No, no, I can do this. For sure. I'm highly motivated for the console in the summer."

"Okay, but for the record, my suggestion would be to extend your timeline and save at a pace that is much more realistic with money you are much more certain will come in."

"Noted," he said. "But I got this. I just can't wait."

I smiled. "Alright. Any other questions for the plan?" I asked.

"I need to know how I actually do this when I get the money. Like, sometimes I get $60 and other times $10 for a lawn. I get the numbers overall, but what do I do when I actually get paid? Where do I put the money?"

"Great question!" I said enthusiastically. "Do you have a chequing account?"

He let out a sigh. "I do, but I actually hate using it."

"Why?" I was surprised.

"I get paid in all cash for my jobs. No one e-transfers me. Weird, eh? So, I have to go down to the bank to deposit it and I usually spend it before I actually get there. It just ends up being a pain for how I'm paid and the kinds of transactions I make."

"Gotcha," I said. "How do you save right now?"

He smiled. "I just put everything into a Mason jar in my sock drawer, remember?" He looked sheepish. "I know that's not smart."

I smiled. "Listen, building a savings and spending habit, no matter how you do it, is good. You don't need to feel bad. If you are always paid in cash, and an online account or app isn't your thing, that's okay. The thing you're giving up is the convenience of using a debit card or prepaid card and also the potential interest."

"I thought I was too young to open a high-interest savings account."*

"You are right now, but things are always changing in the financial technology landscape in Canada. So I bet there will be some sort of solution to this for youth soon."

"So in the meantime, I can keep using my Mason jar?"

"Yep. But use three. Minimum."

"What do I need three for?"

"You're essentially mimicking your future bank accounts."

I brought out a piece of paper and drew three big circles on it.

"Label the first one short-term savings." I put that in the first circle. "This is where you'll save for your console. Short-term savings is money that you 'save' in order to spend on something big later. It's not real savings because it's not improving your financial future. It's spending money that you'll stash and spend later. Make sense?"

He nodded. "Got it."

"Label the second one long-term savings." I wrote that in the next circle.

"Let me guess," David said. "That's savings that improves your financial future?"

I gave him the wink and the finger gun because I'm a dork. "You got it. Money here would be for school, a future house, retirement savings, stuff like that."

"I don't have any of that right now," he said. "Is that bad?"

I shook my head. "Not at all. It's normal at your age. But this is about setting you up with good financial habits now. So, if you plan on post-secondary, you may want to sit down with your parents and figure out what you need to save up for school or if you plan on using loans in a few years."

He grimaced. "I can't even think about that right now."

"You're young. There's time. But it may be a good idea to get that conversation going so that you know if you should be putting some money aside in the long-term savings jar sooner rather than later."

"And what's the last one?"

"Spending money!" I said excitedly and wrote that in big letters in the third circle. "This is the portion of your money that is meant to be enjoyed and spent to afford your daily life!"

He smiled. "The fun money."

"Exactly. And it's helpful to organize this way. With three jars in front of you, you can see the money you can spend between now and the next time you get paid."

"I like it."

"Good!"

"But how do I decide what goes in which jar when I get paid? For example, I have $20 in there now, plus $30 in my wallet, and then I'll get $60 on Thursday."

I thought about it for a moment. "When money comes to you in different amounts, the best thing to do is save a certain percentage each time you get paid."

"Like the 50–50 rule?" he asked. "Every time I get money, half goes to spending and half goes to savings?"

"I actually think that's a great idea for you, but you won't reach your savings timeline goal by only putting away 50%."

He scrunched his face. "Why not?"

"If you have $20 in current savings plus $30 in current earnings and a Future Income of $520, that adds up to $570. Half of that would only be $285 saved and $285 spent. You won't have enough for the game console by the end of July to hit your savings target of August 1st."

"What percentage do I use to hit my spending goal of $140?" he asked.

"You tell me," I said with a smile.

"Okay! So, I divide the $140 I want to go to the spending jar by $570, the total income I have over the period."

"Yes."

"So, $140 divided by $570 is . . ." He punched the numbers into the calculator. "It's 24.5%. So I can only spend 25% of my income if I want to save enough by the end of July."

"Right." I held up the page with the circles. "Which means that every time you get paid, 25% of it goes to the spending jar and the rest goes to the short-term savings jar. None to the long-term savings jar yet."

He nodded and typed a note into his phone. "When I get $60 from babysitting Olivia, I multiply that by 0.25 or 25%, and that goes to the spending jar."

"Yes."

"So that would be $15 to spending and $45 to short-term savings (0.25 x $60)."

"Correct."

"And the $20 I have in there now, I'd put $5 of it to spending (0.25 x $20)."

"You got it."

He nodded and lowered the phone. "I like it."

I set the page aside and leaned in. "Again, for the record, I think this plan is too tight. Maybe the 50–50 rule would be more realistic with a longer timeline of three to four months."

"I know. But I think I can make this work."

"Want to touch base in late July and see where you're at?" I asked. "I'd love to know how it all plays out."

"Yeah, for sure. But I have one last question."

"What's up?"

"Do adults use this sort of banking plan? Like, not jars, but a spending account, a short-term savings account, and a long-term savings account?"

"The financially savvy ones do! Spending accounts are chequing accounts. Where day-to-day transactions happen, where your debit card is attached, and where you'd pay off a credit card from. A chequing account is the spending jar."

"What about the short-term savings?"

"That's more like a regular savings account at a bank. Nothing fancy, but maybe it earns a little interest (we tackle this in Part 5). The money is stashed in there for a short time, ready to be spent down the road. Many people have three short-term savings accounts."

I listed them and wrote them down: travel/trips, emergency, big purchases.

"And they'd put money in those accounts every payday or something?"

"Yep. Stashing money to be spent later on big things."

He nodded in approval. "What about the long-term? Is that like RRSPs and stuff?"

"Absolutely! The long-term savings is money that goes to RRSPs* (Registered Retirement Savings Plans), TFSAs* (Tax-Free Savings Accounts), and even paying down a mortgage or saving for a house. Any of the accounts that will help you build your financial future."

"I like thinking about my money this way." He picked up the page with the circles. "Spending here. Big spending there. Don't spend until you're old there."

I stood up and we walked to the door together. "Keep me posted, okay?"

He grinned on his way out. "You bet."

I couldn't help smiling as I watched him walk away. I was so excited for him to have his new spending and savings jars and was really curious to see if he could meet his August timeline. Stay tuned for Part 3 when we follow up with David!

CHAPTER 5 NITTY GRITTY

What Is a High-Interest Savings Account (HISA)?

- A HISA is a bank account where you earn more interest than you would in a chequing account.

- Historically, you must be the age of majority to open one on your own. However, that may be changing as you read this! New fintech companies are starting to make this possible for younger people (see: https://www.neofinancial.com/youth/hisa). Do your research. It's possible youth under the age of majority are able to get some interest!

- Just make sure the account is CDIC insured. We tackle that in Part 5.

- For more information, read https://www.canada.ca/en/financial -consumer-agency/services/banking/bank-accounts/savings -account.html.

What Is a Registered Retirement Savings Plan (RRSP)?

- An RRSP is a savings account that you can also invest in (when you're older).

- The money that goes into the RRSP is tax deductible. That means, when you save money in there, you pay less tax that year.

- It is also tax sheltered, which means the money that you earn on the account is not taxed as long as the money remains in the account.

- When you take money out, it's taxable, so once you put money in there, you want to keep it there unless it's for your first-time home or full-time schooling.

- Technically, there's no minimum age required to open an RRSP. However, you must have a job, and have earned an income, and gotten a T4 from your employer in the previous tax year to qualify. In addition, you may have a hard time finding a financial institution that will let you open an RRSP before you reach the age of majority for your province.

- For more information, read https://www.canada.ca/en/revenue -agency/services/tax/individuals/topics/rrsps-related-plans /registered-retirement-savings-plan-rrsp.html.

What Is a Tax-Free Savings Account (TFSA)?

- A TFSA is a savings account that you can also invest in when you are an adult.

- It's also a tax shelter, which means the money that you earn (interest, dividends, or capital gains) is not taxed as long as the money is in the account.

- It is NOT a tax deduction the way the RRSP is.

- When you take money out, it is NOT taxable to you, unlike the RRSP. So you could save money here and then take it out for something other than a first-time home or school, and you would still not pay tax.

- You must be the age of majority to open a TFSA. But if you live in a province where the age of majority is 19, you accumulate room in the TFSA starting at age 18!

- For more information, read https://www.canada.ca/en/revenue -agency/services/tax/individuals/topics/tax-free-savings-account .html.

Do You Know Your Stuff?

Test your knowledge with these True or False questions.

QUESTION 1: Your savings targeted timeline is the amount of time you want it to take between now and reaching your goal. *True.*

QUESTION 2: Short-term savings is money that you spend that month.

False. Short-term savings is money that you *save* in order to spend on something big later. It's not real savings because it's not improving your financial future.

QUESTION 3: Long-term savings is money that you save so that you can spend it on a big purchase in a year.

False. Long-term savings is savings that improves your financial future.

QUESTION 4: Ketchup goes in the pantry.

False. Once opened, always in the fridge. ☺

QUESTION 5: When income is unpredictable in timing or amounts, it's best to put money aside in percentages rather than dollar amounts. *True.*

HOMEWORK

Jamie and Bailey have three jars: short-term, long-term, and spending money. They are self-employed and their money comes in at weird times in different amounts. Their targeted savings timeline is three months.

Their projected income over the three months is $1,200. Their projected expenses over this timeline is $825. They have to save $150 over three months to short-term savings and $225 to long-term savings.

Calculate the percentage of income that goes into each jar each time they get paid.

Solution:

TO LONG-TERM SAVINGS: $225/$1,200 = 18.75% each time they get paid

TO SHORT-TERM SAVINGS: $150/$1,200 = 12.5% each time they get paid

TO SPENDING MONEY: $825/$1,200 = 68.75%

6

Tania, Who Wants to Graduate University with Zero Debt

AGE:	17 (almost 18)
SIBLING STATUS:	Has a younger brother
INCOME SOURCE:	Part-time job at the local arena
REGULAR INCOME CALCULATION:	$760 in the next 4 weeks
CURRENT SAVINGS:	$2,500 in savings account

During our first meeting, we calculated Tania's projected income for the time between now and school and helped her figure out if giving up the time for work was worth it or not. She was still keen to get through the question list.

Tania reshared her screen with the questions she had sent in to me. She put a strike through the first two.

"Now on to question three. How much do I actually need to put aside so I am not in debt forever?"

I let out a big breath. "That's a big question."

"I know. That's why I need your help."

I nodded and smiled. "The first thing we need to do is flush out what your actual goals are."

"Simple," she said. "I don't want to go into debt."

"For sure. But that's a big umbrella. There may be other short-term savings goals we need to think about too."

I watched her tense up. "What do you mean?"

"Imagine three buckets of money: spending money, short-term savings, and long-term savings. Spending money is what you need to spend on daily life."

"Things like transit, food I pay for, clothes I pay for, and so on?"

"Exactly."

"Well, that's not really a savings goal. Spending money is not savings," Tania said.

"No, it's not, but the more spending money someone needs, the less they have for saving, so expenses matter."

She nodded. "What's the difference between short-term and long-term savings? Is school tuition short-term savings because it's happening soon?"

I shook my head. "Great question, but no. Short-term savings isn't really about how long it takes until you reach your goal. It's actually money that will be spent on something that won't improve your financial future. For example, saving up to buy a concert ticket. You save money, so it's not spending money, but you plan on spending it down the road on something that won't improve your finances. Even though it may improve your life," I said with a smile.

"But tuition doesn't really improve my finances. Like, school costs money. It's not an investment."

"School is absolutely an investment!"

"But my bank accounts will be empty by the end of school. How is that long-term savings?"

"The biggest asset in anyone's life is their Future Income. It is the most important piece of all future finances. Remember how we just forecasted your Future Income over the next 20 months until school starts?"

She nodded.

"Now imagine you had no income. We wouldn't have gotten very far."

"True."

"So, we know that going to school, or taking career training certificates, or learning a skill or a trade are all things that cost money. But you spend that money now in order to improve your chances of being paid a higher Future Income. Education, most of the time in this economy, improves your long-term finances. In other words, any money you're saving now to spend on something that improves your Future Income is a form of long-term savings, not short-term savings. Does that make sense?"

She relaxed and nodded slowly. "Yes. Because I can't save a lot of money in the future if I don't make enough money to pay my bills and save."

"Exactly."

"And I can't make more money if I don't go to school to try and land a higher paying job."

"You got it."

"Okay. Yeah, I see that."

I smiled. "So, let's figure out how much money you would need in order to avoid going into debt during your first year at school."

She let out a big breath. "I'm scared."

"I get that. Post-secondary does not come cheap, which is why we need to be realistic about the financial side of things."

She nodded so solemnly for a girl her age I felt my heart squeeze.

"Let's start by estimating the total cost of going to school," I said. "From start to finish."

"Yikes." She smiled a little. "I actually don't know if I can look at it."

"Don't be scared. It may not be as bad as you think. How long is your program?"

"Four years."

"Four years. That's your targeted savings timeline for this exercise. Now, let's map out all the total costs you're likely to face in order to plan how much you'd like to have in savings. In an ideal world."

I made a chart and shared my screen with her.

"How much is tuition each year?"

"$10,000."

I wrote "$40,000" ($10,000 x 4 years) in the spreadsheet.

"Books?"

"About $2,500 per year I've been told."

"Are you living on campus?" I asked.

She let out a laugh. "Yeah, right. It's so expensive. No, I'll be commuting and living at home for free."

"Transit will definitely increase the amount you need for daily spending money while you're in school. But what about other spending money while you're there? Food, life. Dare I say, fun?"

She frowned. "I can't afford fun."

"I get that it feels that way. But you're so young. Maybe there's a little bit of wiggle room."

"Well, right now I don't spend anything. Like, nothing."

"I'm sure you spend some money. How did you get here today?"

"I biked."

"When did you buy those pants?"

She smiled. "Okay, I bought pants, like, a year ago."

"But at some point you're going to have to buy pants again. Shoes again. These things will happen."

"Yes. But I really don't spend a lot." She shared her screen with me again and showed me an app that tracks her spending.

"See?"

I looked and realized she was right. She really didn't spend much.

"You just spent over $5,000 last year including transit, food, entertainment, and clothing."

"Yes. Not much. Life is so expensive. Every time I get paid $190.08 per week, I give myself $101.08 for the week for all my spending, and I save $89 each week. It's very specific, I know."

"You could round up."

She shook her head. "No, I want to know what I can spend and save to the dollar."

Noted.

"I usually factor in a few weeks of vacation where I don't get paid. So approximately $5,000 per year of spending money makes sense."

"Do you think that's sustainable while you're at school?" I asked.

"I think it has to be."

"If nothing changes," I said, "that adds up to $70,000 for all four years with minimum spending money. That's the long-term savings goal. It's a big one."

Estimated Costs for University

COSTS	ESTIMATED AMOUNT
Tuition	$40,000 ($10,000 x 4 years)
Books	$10,000 ($2,500 x 4 years)
Residence	$0 (living at home)
Spending money	$20,000 ($5,000 x 4 years)
TOTAL	$70,000

She sat there quiet for a moment.

"Tania?" I asked.

She sounded on the verge of tears. "How do people do this? How are we supposed to make this work if we don't have rich parents? I'm probably gonna have to go into massive debt and probably graduate with a job that won't even allow me to pay it off until I'm 40."

"I know it's a lot. But honestly, you may actually be able to make a big dent here because you're working full-time while living at home next year."

"Do you think I'll have enough?"

"Let's see! Remember that in Phase 1, when you're part-time, you'll earn $760.32 a month and save $356 per month for school, which is $89 per weekly pay. You'll do this for six months until the end of June."

I calculated. "That's $2,136 ($356 x 6 months) while you're part-time, before graduating. Then, for 14 months, this July to next September, you'll be full-time, earning $2,248 a month. If you could save $1,830 each month, when you're full-time, you'll save up $25,620 ($1,830 x 14 months)."

I was getting excited.

"Right."

"So, if you keep spending the same way, the $5,000 a year, you'll have $27,756 ($2,136 in Phase 1 + $25,620 in Phase 2) saved by the time school starts!"

"That's not even half of what I need while I'm in school," she said, almost instantly. "It's $70,000."

"Yeah, but you'll also be working part-time while you're in school, right?"

"Oh yeah. Taking home $14.05 an hour after tax for five hours a week. I don't think I can work more than one shift a week when I'm in school. But then full-time in the summer again for four months each year."

"Exactly!" I said. "Watch this." I pointed to the chart. "Part-time work while in school would be 36 weeks of the year, five hours a week at $14.05. The other 16 weeks (52 weeks in a year less 36 while in school) would be full-time at $14.05 for 40 hours a week each year."

"Well, I wouldn't work every week of the year. Probably 34 weeks while in school. I'd take the holidays and reading week. Maybe 14 weeks in the summer. I would take some vacation too."

I wrote it all in the spreadsheet.

Tania's Projected Future Income Calculation while in University

Income Source	Random	Predictable	Reoccurring	Included in Regular Income	Taxable? What rate?	A — Predictable Income amount after tax $	B — How many times in the next 34 weeks?	C — Total Future Income for next 34 weeks (A x B)
Part-time job		X	X	Yes	16.11%	$14.05 (100%– 16.11%) x $16.75	170 (5 hours x 34 weeks)	$2,388
Full-time job		X	X	Yes	16.11%	$14.05 (100%– 16.11%) x $16.75	560 (40 hours x 14 weeks)	$7,868
TOTAL								$10,256

"Your projected income in school is $10,256 per year. That's $41,024 ($10,256 x 4) over the four years!"

She smiled and leaned closer to the screen. "Okay, tell me more."

"Heading into school, you'd have $27,756 saved up. Plus the $2,500 you already saved is $30,256."

She nodded.

"Then you'd make $41,024 over the four years you're there."

"Right."

"That's $71,280! Tania! You need $70,000! That's almost exactly what you need! No shortfall!"

I put it all into a chart so she could see the year-by-year cash flow.

"Look at this. You start school with $30,256, then you spend $12,500 a year between $10,000 tuition and $2,500 for books. Then, you still spend your $5,000 a year for spending money and you keep adding the $10,256 to your savings account when you get paid! It works!"

Tania's Long-Term Savings Goals

	LONG-TERM SAVINGS	SCHOOL EXPENSES	SPENDING MONEY	LONG-TERM SAVINGS BALANCE
BEFORE-SCHOOL SAVINGS	$30,256 ($356 x 6 + $1,830 x 14 + $2,500)			$30,256
YEAR 1	+$10,256 (from income)	-$12,500	-$5,000	$23,012
YEAR 2	+$10,256 (from income)	-$12,500	-$5,000	$15,768
YEAR 3	+$10,256 (from income	-$12,500	-$5,000	$8,524
YEAR 4	+$10,256 (from income)	-$12,500	-$5,000	$1,280

She didn't say anything. She just looked at it. I couldn't tell if she was excited or upset.

"Tania. When we map it out year by year like this, you actually did it!"

She still didn't say anything, and she didn't look thrilled.

"These are just rough estimates." I started talking quickly, trying to show her that she was doing such an excellent job. "And we haven't taken any emergencies into account. But this is so close to what you'll need, I think you can feel really good that you're not going to be swimming in debt after school if the spending estimates and the work assumptions are correct."

"That's good," she said.

"Yet you don't seem so excited."

"I am. But also not."

"How so?"

"I just work so hard. I spend barely anything. I guess I hoped that I'd have enough that I could also go on my grad trip, but if these are the numbers, I definitely can't."

"What grad trip?"

"There's a trip that all my pals are going on to Bermuda for a week. My grandmother still lives there. She's not well. I haven't been back for years because we couldn't afford it. I'd love to go, but it would cost $5,000 between flights and the resort and everything. Plus, I'd need to rent a car to get to my grandmother's place and extend my trip. I was going to use the $2,500 I already have saved up, but I thought there'd be more savings so that I didn't have to eat into my school savings."

"I see the math, but I think that maybe you can still do all of it. You're saving so much and lots can change over the next four years."

"Are you telling me to go into debt?"

Eek! "No, I'm saying these forecasts, this projected income and savings, are just that. Forecasts. Projections. Estimates. Maybe you earn a little more in year three. Maybe you spend less in year four. It's a rough estimate to see if you're saving enough and on the right track."

"But in the next year, if I go on this trip, I won't have enough for all my tuition, living, and transit based on those numbers. I already watch everything I spend. I'd have to borrow the rest."

I thought about that. She was right. Some portion of it would have to come from debt.

"I'm sure there's a way you could earn it back over time," I said.

She shook her head and sat back from the screen again. "No. I don't want to pay interest. I don't want to be in debt. My parents have been in debt their whole lives, and they are always stressed out. I'm not going to do it. This is how it starts. Stuff like this."

She was resolute.

"Tania," I said gently. "Just because your parents are in debt doesn't mean that you will be."

She thought for a moment. "What if I don't spend anything between now and July? That's 24 paycheques, where I could save the $101.08 a week I usually spend. Then, I'd have the extra $2,425.92 ($101.08 x 24) plus the $2,500 in savings already. That would be enough for me to pay for the trip and still save the $89 a week, the $356 a month, that I'm supposed to save for school, right?"

"Yes, but Tania, you already barely spend money. I'm not sure reducing spending to $0 for six months is realistic. What about your phone, and the subscriptions you pay for?"

She slumped. "Right. But that stuff is only, like, 133 bucks a month." I heard her clicking through something on her screen and then she shared her own spreadsheet with me. "Okay, I make $190.08 each payday, every week right now until the end of June, and I put aside $89 for school savings and I usually keep the rest ($101.08) for my spending. Of that $101.08, $33.25 each week ($133/4 weeks) is to pay for bills and subscriptions and I keep $67.83 for spending money for groceries and life. But what if I don't spend any spending money? Like, no shopping, no meals out, and I put the $67.83 aside for the trip?"

I grimaced. "Are you sure that's realistic for six months? No spending money?"

"It is," she said with conviction. "I can totally do it. I live at home. I don't need expensive things, and this trip means a lot to me. I haven't seen my grandmother in a long time. Plus, a trip with my friends. We are all going to separate places for university. My two best friends are moving away and may not even come back in the summers."

I didn't say anything. I didn't want to burst her bubble, but no-spending-money plans rarely work.

She looked down. "I really want to go."

I let out a big breath. If anyone could do it, it was Tania.

"If you can manage it," I said, "that would get you close. You'd save up around $1,600-ish." I quickly did the calculation. "$1,627.92 to be exact ($67.83 x 24 weeks). That extra would mean you'd have $4,127 saved up by the first week of July. The $2,500 in savings from before and $1,627. Would that do it?"

She beamed. "I think so. I'm definitely going to try. I know it's not the $5,000, but maybe I can stick four of us in a hotel room. Or not rent a car to keep costs really low, or find some other way to keep it within that price range."

"So, six months is your targeted savings timeline."

"Yes. The trip is the first week of July."

"So $190.08 comes in for 24 weeks. You put $33.25 aside for your bills. You put $89 aside for your long-term savings goal for school, and you save $67.83 per week to short-term savings for the trip instead of spending it."

"Awesome. Done," she said.

This was the most excited I'd seen her.

"I'm worried," I told her.

"I can do it," she said. "I promise."

"I don't agree that it's realistic, but I'm happy to make the plan because you seem very motivated."

"So I need a new savings account?"

"Technically, you need two. One for long-term school savings and one for the trip. A long-term savings account and a short-term savings account."

"Can I do this next week? I turn 18."

"Happy early birthday! You definitely can. Open two savings accounts. One that you can name short-term savings and the second you can name long-term savings."

"But I still keep my chequing account. The one where my weekly pay goes, with my debit card and everything."

"Oh, yes. And normally, you'd leave the $67.83 in there for spending each payday."

"So $190.08 comes in. I move $67.83 to short-term savings, leave $33.25 in my chequing account, and move $89 to long-term savings for 24 weeks."

"That's right."

"Then re-evaluate in 24 weeks in July once I've achieved my short-term goal for the trip."

"Exactly. In 24 weeks you should have $4,127—$2,500 existing savings plus $1,627 ($67.83 x 24) of trip savings—in short-term savings and $2,136 ($89 x 24) in long-term savings for school."

"What's the benefit of all these accounts, though? Don't they cost me bank fees?"

"Some don't. You could sign up for savings accounts at banks that don't have any bank fees. Even if this is outside of your usual financial institution. Having separate accounts is extremely helpful for our money mindset. When you see money building up in an account dedicated to something specific, it's very motivating. Plus, it ensures that it's not in a chequing account and accidentally spent."

We ended our session for the day and planned to meet up in six months to make a new savings plan for once the trip happened.

I wished Tania luck, and I was rooting for her. However, vowing to spend no money doesn't usually end well because it's not realistic. I was worried, but also excited to see her in 24 weeks.

Do You Know Your Stuff?

Test your knowledge with these True or False questions.

QUESTION 1: The biggest asset in anyone's life is their Future Income. *True.*

QUESTION 2: You always have to pay bank fees to have a chequing account.

False. Many banking plans have no fees.

QUESTION 3: Expenses don't matter when calculating a savings plan.

False. There are always expenses you have to pay. The more expenses, the less you can save.

QUESTION 4: Saving money feels good! *True!*

QUESTION 5: Your savings is your projected income minus your projected expenses. *True.*

HOMEWORK

Choose long-term and short-term savings goals and calculate whether you can afford them.

STEP 1: Set a short-term savings goal.

STEP 2: Set a long-term savings goal.

The two goals may have different timelines, for example, $400 in 10 months for short-term savings, and $1,200 a year for long-term savings (12 months).

STEP 3: Figure out how much you need to save each month/week/year to hit your goal.

$400/10 months = $40 per month for 10 months to short-term savings

$1,200/12 months = $100 per month for 12 months to long-term savings

STEP 4: Calculate your projected income over that time period.

Projected Future Income Calculation

Timeline

Income Source	Random	Predictable	Reoccurring	Included in Regular Income	Taxable? What rate?	A — Predictable Income amount after tax $	B — How many times in the next X weeks?	C — Total Future Income for next X weeks (A x B)
Part-time job								
Full-time job								
TOTAL								

STEP 5: Calculate your projected expenses over that period. More on this in Part 3, but you can estimate for now.

STEP 6: Calculate whether you can afford your savings goals.

Example

STEP 1: Outline your targeted savings timeline (e.g., three months).

STEP 2: Calculate how much you need to save (e.g., $150 in three months to short-term savings and $225 in three months to long-term savings).

STEP 3: Figure out how much you need to save each month/week/year to hit your goal.

$150/3 months = $50 a month to short-term savings

$225/3 months = $75 a month to long-term savings

STEP 4: Calculate projected income over that time period.

For example, if someone worked five hours a week for $20 an hour after deductions, four weeks each month, for three months:

Timeline						A	B	C
Income Source	Random	Predictable	Reoccurring	Included in Regular Income	Taxable? What rate?	Predictable Income amount after tax $	How many times in the next X weeks?	Total Future Income for next X weeks (A x B)
Part-time job		X	X	Yes	No	$20 x 5 = $100	12 weeks	$100 x 12 = $1,200'
Full-time job								
TOTAL								$1,200

They will earn $1,200 over three months, or $400 a month ($1,200/3).

STEP 5: Calculate your projected expenses over that period.

If someone spends the following each month for three months:

> $125 takeout lunches
> $50 cellphone
> $100 shopping

$275 a month x 3 months = $825 in total projected expenses over that period

STEP 6: Calculate whether you can afford it.

Projected income over targeted savings period ($1,200) – projected expenses over targeted savings period ($825) = $375.

SHORT-TERM GOAL: $150

LONG-TERM GOAL: $225

$375 – $150 – $225 = $0. No shortfall.

This works!

7

Mia, Who Needed to Put Her Raise to Work

AGE:	13
SIBLING STATUS:	Middle kid between two sisters
INCOME SOURCE:	Has a regular allowance
REGULAR INCOME CALCULATION:	$100 in the next 4 weeks
CURRENT SAVINGS:	$0 anywhere

I met with Mia again about two weeks after our first meeting. Her mom, Sofia, had set it up after Mia asked for a raise. The two of them sat down on the other side of my desk.

Sofia did not waste time. "Shannon, I didn't expect Mia to ask for a raise after meeting you."

Mia and I shared a grin.

"Sorry 'bout that!" I joked.

Fortunately, Sofia smiled too. "It's okay. It's good, actually. I was so impressed with how she did it and the argument she made that I agreed to a six-month trial. If she can show me that she can actually save, I'm happy to keep it permanently, including the bonus chores."

Mia nodded.

"That's great," I said. "So, what do you want to get out of this session today?"

Sofia gestured for Mia to answer.

Mia looked me in the eye. "I need a savings plan."

Sofia nodded. "I want her to learn how to save money."

"It's really great to learn those habits now while you're young. Doesn't matter if it's $2 or $200 a month, the habit of saving is what matters."

"Exactly," Sofia said and stood up. "I'll be in the waiting room."

Once Sofia left, I turned to smile at Mia. "Nicely done!"

She grinned. "I'm so happy about it. I thought she'd say no for sure. But I had everything mapped out like you said. I showed the comparison to my peers, the money I was saving her by doing some bonus chores, and the inflation chart. She loved it!"

"I'm so glad. This is a wonderful experience that you can use when you're older too. With a real job."

"I never thought about earning more. It's wild, but it never even crossed my mind."

"But now we have to start saving some money," I said.

Her nod was firm, determined. "We do."

"Did you get any closer to the dress?" I asked.

She shrugged. "No. My raise only kicked in last Friday and I had to spend one bonus chore already on a birthday gift for a pal."

"Then let's start by outlining your short-term versus long-term savings goals," I said.

She got out her blue pen and notebook. "Okay. What are my long-term goals?"

I smiled. "Mia, I can't tell you that. They're not my goals, they're yours."

She giggled. "That makes sense." She thought for a moment. "Do you mean long-term savings like the dress I want? Because it takes a long time to save for it?"

"Not exactly," I said and leaned toward her. "The dress is actually a short-term savings goal. Short-term savings is money that you save up but only so you can spend it on something big later. Even if we save for your dress, when you buy it, there won't be any long-term financial gain. Does that make sense?"

She nodded. "I'm saving because I'm not spending it that day, but it's meant to be spent later."

"Exactly."

"So long-term savings is money that I put away and don't spend. Which makes it good for my future?"

"Yes!" I said. "Things like schooling, a house, retirement. That kind of thing."

"Do other 13-year-olds have long-term savings? Am I, like, the only one who doesn't?"

I laughed. "Not at all. It would be rare for a 13-year-old to be saving for the long term at this point in your life because there isn't a lot of money to save."

"What's the point if I don't have much to save anyway?"

"The point is that time is on your side. Saving even a small amount regularly will make a huge difference in the long run."

She looked skeptical, so I took out my pen. "Let's use the $200 dress as an example. Imagine you wanted to have $100 by grad."

"I'm not really imagining. I'm hoping that's true!"

"So, your targeted savings timeline is four months because there are four months from now until grad."

She nodded.

"If you started today, you'd have to save $25 a month ($100/4 months)."

"That doesn't sound too bad," she said, "if I get some bonus chores."

"But what if you didn't start saving for another month? How many months would you have left to save?"

"Three."

"With only three months left to save, you'd have to save $33.33 a month ($100/3 months). See the difference?"

She nodded. "The shorter the timeline, the higher the actual dollar amount I have to save each month."

"Exactly. It's the same with long-term retirement savings. When someone starts young, like in their early twenties, they have 45 years to save until they are 65 years old. At that stage, even a little bit can go a long way. On the other hand, someone starting to save for retirement at age 50 only has 15 years left to save and has to put aside a lot each month. Does that make sense?"

"It does. So, should I be saving for retirement now?"

I smiled. "No. You have a lot of time for that. Right now, the big long-term savings plan I'd focus on for you, if any, would be money to pay for any post-secondary education or certificates you'll need to help get you a job that pays a living wage. The other long-term savings stuff can't happen if you don't have an income to save when you grow up."

"And make my millions," she said, matching my smile.

"Precisely."

"Well, I don't think I have enough money to save for short-term savings and long-term right now. Maybe when I'm older in high school and I can get a part-time job that pays more than allowance. Is that okay?"

"Of course that's okay. We'll make a new plan when you're older! You'll have all the skills."

"Great. If I just put my new $5 raise a week into my savings and add two bonus chores, I can get my dress by June."

"Pretty much! This is a good tip when you're a grown-up too. Any time you get a raise, try to only spend what you used to make for your daily life, and save the raise each payday. It helps avoid something called lifestyle inflation."

"What's that? The same inflation that we talked about last time? How the prices go up?"

"Not exactly. Lifestyle inflation is when you make more money, so you buy more things instead of living the same way. It's not really about prices, more about spending more because you have it."

She nodded. "Like if I get a part-time job next year and start going out for $15 lunches every day because I can."

"Right."

She pointed a finger at me. "That's a really good tip."

"I think so too!"

She wrote it down in her blue notebook.

"I've got another one for you," I said.

"Awesome," she said, pen at the ready.

"You could mimic something called payroll deductions for your new savings."

She scrunched her face. "What are payroll deductions?"

"Payroll deductions are savings that come right off your paycheque and into your savings before you even get a chance to see it. When you have a job that deposits your salary directly into a chequing account, an employer may automatically take the amount of money you want to save off your paycheque and put it into a savings account for you. Then, only the money you can spend goes into your chequing account."

"I don't have a job yet."

"That's okay. Technically, your mom is your employer if you're getting an allowance."

"Go on," she said, but I could tell she was a little leery about where I was going with this.

"You get your allowance on Fridays, right?"

She nodded.

"And it's now $25 a week plus bonus money?"

Another nod.

"You could have your mom give you the $20 each Friday, like it used to be. And get her to set the spending limit on your banking app to $20. That will hold back the $5 into savings. You're sort of faking a payroll deduction."

She thought about that for a moment, then smiled. "My mom would just *love* that."

We laughed together.

"I'm serious, though. Payroll deductions or automatic savings can be an amazing savings accelerator because you are never tempted to spend the money you want to save because it's never in your hands. People also do this with automatic savings withdrawals. Like, on payday, they have an automatic withdrawal set up so that money comes in but is basically gone right away. The point is that you never really have access to the money that is earmarked for savings."

"Sounds okay," she said, but there was no enthusiasm for the plan. I tried another route.

"Think about it this way," I said. "With just $5 every week plus two bonus chores for $10 each, you'll reach $100 for the dress before you know it. It won't even feel like work."

She sighed. "You're right. I was already excited about what else I could do with the bonus money, but that's not saving, so I get it. I have to pretend it's not there."

I sighed too. Coming to decisions like this was never easy, even when it made sense. But the good news was that Mia was on board for the change.

"I promise it will make saving easier," I said. "You don't have to give it up yourself, and you won't see it in a jar, begging to be spent."

She giggled, coming back to her usual self again. "I just love spending money."

"I mean, who doesn't?"

"My mom!"

We burst out laughing.

Mia left my office with her mom and her new plan to have her $5 raise plus her bonus money automatically taken off her allowance. Her mom promised to save it up and give her the $100 that would be saved over the next four months for the dress. They both left happy and excited to try it out.

Stay tuned for Part 3, when we learn whether Mia was able to stick to her savings plan and get the dress!

Do You Know Your Stuff?

Test your knowledge with these True or False questions.

QUESTION 1: The shorter the targeted savings timeline, the less you have to save each pay period.

False. The shorter the targeted savings timeline, the MORE you have to save each pay period.

QUESTION 2: Lifestyle inflation is when you make more money, so you buy more things instead of living the same way. It's not really about prices, more about spending more because you have it. *True.*

QUESTION 3: Automatic spending withdrawals are an amazing way to save money.

False. Automatic SAVINGS withdrawals. ☺

QUESTION 4: Payroll deductions are savings that come right off your paycheque and into your savings before you even get a chance to see it. *True.*

QUESTION 5: You can't have payroll deductions unless you have a job with an employer.

True. However, you CAN pretend to, by either having a parent/caregiver withhold some of your allowance or setting up automatic savings withdrawals.

HOMEWORK

- Set up automated savings of some sort.

- Maybe you do this with an allowance by asking your parent/caregiver to withhold an amount of money you'd like to save.

- Maybe you have a chequing account for spending and a savings account. Set up an automatic savings withdrawal on payday to move an amount you want to save from chequing to savings.

- Fill out the money reflection below after three months.

The first three automatic withdrawals made me feel:

_____

_____

_____

Did it feel easier to save because the money earmarked for savings never actually came to me?

_____

_____

_____

Did I hit my savings target?

_____

_____

_____

Oliver, Who Did All the Sneaking Around

AGE:	16
SIBLING STATUS:	Only child
INCOME SOURCE:	Not allowed to have a job because he needs to keep his grades up; doesn't need an allowance because he can "get money from my parents whenever I ask"
REGULAR INCOME:	Should be $100 a month (fingers crossed)
CURRENT SAVINGS:	$500 in an online chequing account; an RESP for university (if he gets in); a stock simulator account* with $5,000 in it—Oliver makes stock trades to practise, then his dad executes the trades for real in an online investment account that Oliver will have access to when he's 18

hen Oliver left my office after our first meeting, he had a plan to talk to his father about allowing him to spend $25 a week, no questions asked. I was nervous for him and was looking forward to this next meeting to see how things went.

"Hey, Oliver," I said as he entered the room. He didn't have his basketball this time.

"Hey." He sat down with a gloomy look on his face.

"Still a good day to do the session?" I asked.

"Oh, yeah. All good."

I didn't believe this, but hoped that our second session wasn't the buzzkill.

"I've been really excited to follow up with you. How did the hard money conversation go with your parents? About the $100 a month?"

He grimaced. "Yeah. Well, I didn't really do it. I'm sorry."

"Hey, that's okay," I assured him. "Is that why you don't seem as excited to see me?"

He smiled. "Sort of. I just feel bad I didn't do what we planned."

"Hey, no worries. Truly. It was an idea. An experiment. In fact, this is actually a really great learning moment for you when it comes to money management."

"Oh yeah?" He raised his eyebrows.

"Sure!" I said. "Experiments with budgets and money talks go wrong all the time or don't even get started. Knowing what you should do with your money and actually doing it are two very different things. You're experiencing that for the first time." I held out a fake microphone like an interviewer. "And how does that feel?" I said in a deep voice.

He cracked a smile and shrugged. "I dunno. I feel like such a baby."

I put the fake microphone away. "What do you mean?"

He sighed. "Like, what's the point? My dad is actually a really nice guy. It's not like I'm scared of him or something, but I just don't know how to do this. He can make me feel so greedy and ungrateful complaining to him when he's got all this money put aside. Like a spoiled brat, you know?"

"I don't think you're spoiled for wanting to use a reasonable amount of your spending money."

He sat back.

"How do you think your dad would feel if you told him what you just told me?" I asked.

He shrugged. "I honestly don't know. He'd probably be sad that I was worried."

I nodded and we sat in silence for a moment. Then I piped up. "How'd you get by the last month?" I asked. "Financially, I mean."

He closed his eyes and shook his head. "See, that's the thing."

"I'm listening."

He tsked at himself and took a big breath. "I didn't ask for money. I just took it out. In cash."

"The $100?"

He nodded. "Yeah."

"How did you manage that? I thought you didn't have access to the debit card."

He went beet red. "I took it from my dad." He looked down. "Without asking."

I nodded. "How'd that go over?"

He laughed nervously. "Uh, not so good."

"Yikes."

"Yeah. He obviously noticed the $100 cash gone and then totally freaked out."

"About the $100 coming out or about the taking the card without asking?"

"Both, I think. Mostly the taking the card."

"Not the best way to start an awkward conversation about money," I said, trying to lighten the mood.

"Nope."

"That's a tough spot."

"Now he thinks I'm buying drugs or vaping."

"Uh-oh."

"Yeah. Not good. Because I took the card, he thinks I'm sneaking around and taking cash because I don't want a paper trail of where I spent my money."

"Technically, that's true."

"Yeah, but I'm not buying drugs or vaping. I'm buying lunch!" He got frustrated. "It's so unfair. I'm not a bad kid. Like, why am I stealing a debit card to buy lunch? It doesn't make sense!"

"That sounds really hard, Oliver. I'm sorry."

"It's not your fault my dad went haywire."

I thought for a moment. "Maybe we can go over some ways to have that hard money conversation?" This was me trying to find a solution. "Maybe we can—"

He cut me off. "No. No. I definitely need things to chill out first. My dad is so pissed off at me. They are monitoring me like crazy."

"I get it. Sorry." I paused. "I want to help."

"It's fine. He's just really mad. Not good timing. Maybe we do the session for today and see how things go at the next one."

"Absolutely," I said and cleared my throat in a funny way, pretending to be very serious. "Today's session is all about savings."

"My savings?"

"More like savings goals," I offered. "I want to know more about what you are saving up for in the short term and the long term."

"Short term being money I need in the next few months, and long term being after high school?"

"Sort of. Short-term savings is money that you save up but intend to spend. It's not 'real' savings. Long-term savings is money that you're saving that will better your future finances."

He nodded.

"For grown-ups, short-term savings is things like trips, cars, emergency funds. That kind of thing. Long-term savings is money put aside for things like retirement, paying down a mortgage, investments. That kind of thing."

"Things that increase your net worth," he said.

"Wow!" I exclaimed. "Very good jargon. Yes. Anything that increases your assets, like savings, or decreases your debts is increasing your net worth because your net worth is all your assets minus all your liabilities."

He nodded. "My dad already has me tracking it."

"It's impressive."

"I feel like all I have are long-term savings."

"What do you mean?"

"I have $500 in my chequing account. I have an RESP for university with $60,000 in it, plus the $5,000 my dad invests that I'll get when I'm 18."

"The RESP is for school," I said. "That's definitely long-term money. But what about the money in the stock simulator account? What are you going to use that for when you're 18?"

He thought for a moment. "I'm not really sure. Maybe a house one day? Maybe a big trip or a year off between high school and post-secondary? I guess that's not helpful. A house would be long-term savings and a trip would be short-term savings."

"It's okay not to know. You're very young. Loads of time to decide." He nodded.

"What would you be saving for in the short run—if you had access to the money?"

He was quiet for a moment. Then he said, "Nothing exciting. Probably clothes, concert tickets. Maybe to take someone out on a big date." He blushed a bit. "I'm really into mountain biking too, so maybe a new bike if my dad didn't want to buy it. I dunno. Normal stuff. But for this type of thing, my parents usually pay for it. But I never know." He rubbed his forehead.

"It is a conundrum," I said. "That you have money and don't have to technically save anything, but also can't spend or save anything if you want to. To practise the habit."

"The habit?"

"The habit of saving. It's one of the most important parts of personal finances. The actual act of not spending all your money. Of putting some aside for later. Every financial plan hinges on someone's ability to do this."

"I guess I'm not a good candidate for financial coaching."

"The opposite actually. Your situation is totally unique. It's a good reminder and a lesson that everyone's financial situation is different, even when we are young. When I started researching, I thought that most people your age would be very similar. But it's not the case at all. Just like adults."

All of a sudden, he sat up straighter, looking interested, curious. More like the Oliver who left our first session keen to try something different. "What if we pretend that I actually do have access to money? That I earn my own money. The $100 a month. What would I do with it to practise saving?"

"The first step is to outline how much you need in your savings goal."

"Let's say I want to save up $300 of my own money. In cash."

"Are you saving for something specific in this scenario?"

"Money that I know is there, just in case."

"That's called an emergency fund. It's an amount of money that you put aside to be spent in the short run if something expensive and unexpected happens."

"What kind of emergencies would I have?" he asked.

"Well, it's different for everyone. For an adult, an emergency account is usually for things like an unexpected car repair, someone losing a job, a flood, or a health problem. That kind of thing. It's short-term savings because the money may have to be spent and won't improve your net worth. The main job of an emergency account is to keep you out of debt when you're old enough to have a credit card. If you're an adult, and the laptop that you need for work breaks, and you have $1,000 in an emergency account, you can pay for the laptop without using a credit card. In that way, it helps your net worth. Emergency accounts are special."

"For me, I think the only emergency I'd have is if my dad fully cut me off."

"Which would be like a job loss. For an adult."

"I guess so."

"So, your savings goal is to build an emergency account worth $300."

"Yes."

"And now we have to figure out your targeted savings timeline. How long until you reach your $300 target?"

"As soon as realistically possible."

I winced. "Soon isn't really a goal. We have to get specific. If you earned $100 a month, and spent nothing, you could do that in three months. But that doesn't seem realistic. The main problem here is that you want to spend the $100 a month, right?"

He raised an eyebrow. "What if I earned $150 a month from a new gig? Hypothetically."

"Hypothetically speaking, you could live off the $100 and save the $50. You could be at $300 in six months ($300/$50)."

"What if the money comes in weird amounts or, like, at weird times?"

"Like, unpredictable pay? Like a side hustle?"

"Yeah. Like, unpredictable."

"Totally unpredictable?"

"Yeah. You don't know how much or when, but it probably works out to $150 a month."

"Well, if it was side hustle money that is normally $150 on average in a month, you'd want to save a specific percentage when money did come in. That's the best way to save with unpredictable money. In this case, it would be 33% ($50/150). Every time money came in, you could put 33% into short-term savings, your emergency fund. And the rest to spending."

"That's great!"

"It would be. It would be great to be able to practise saving a percentage of your income for emergencies."

He looked really excited.

"You seem pumped," I said.

"I am. I'm going to try to bring in some extra money. So I can practise this and build that account. It feels good to have a goal."

"Didn't your dad say you couldn't have a side hustle or a job, though?" I asked carefully.

He shrugged. "I'll think of something."

I raised my eyebrow. "Oliver, if your dad already thinks you're sneaking around, more sneaking around is maybe not the best decision."

"I got it under control." He got up out of the chair and headed for the door. "See you in a month, yeah? With $50 in emergency savings?" he added with a smile.

"More important than the $50," I pointed out, "is the hard money conversation that we both know you need to have with your dad by then too."

He nodded. "When it's the right time, I will. I got this."

"Okay, good luck!" I called after him as he left.

CHAPTER 8 NITTY GRITTY

What Is a Stock Simulator Account?

* A stock market simulator allows you to practise what it would be like to invest without investing any real money.

Do You Know Your Stuff?

Test your knowledge with these True or False questions.

QUESTION 1: Your net worth is how much savings you have.

False. Your net worth is the total amount of your assets minus any debts (liabilities) you have.

QUESTION 2: You can increase your net worth by saving money.

True!

QUESTION 3: You can increase your net worth by paying down debt. *True!*

QUESTION 4: An emergency fund is meant for long-term savings.

False. It's an amount of money that you put aside to be spent in the short run if something expensive and unexpected happens.

QUESTION 5: The main job of an emergency account is to keep you out of debt. *True.*

HOMEWORK

Calculate your net worth.

EXAMPLE: A high school student has $100 in cash savings at home, $50 in a chequing account, and $20,000 in a Registered Education Savings Plan their parents have been saving in. The student is too young for a credit card, but they owe their sibling $80. Using the table below, calculate their net worth.

Net Worth Calculator

ASSETS	
Money in jars	
Money in chequing account	
Money in savings accounts	
Money in investment accounts (RRSPs, RESPs, TFSA, Non-Registered Accounts)	
Other money	
Real estate (if you own a house or property)	
Other (e.g., jewellery, artwork)	
Total Assets (A)	
LIABILITIES	
Loans from pals or siblings	
Credit cards	
Line of credit	
Student loan	
Mortgage	
Car loan	
Other	
Total Liabilities (B)	
NET WORTH (A − B)	

Answer

ASSETS	
Money in jars	$100
Money in chequing account	$50
Money in savings accounts	
Money in investment accounts (RRSPs, RESPs, TFSA, Non-Registered Accounts)	$20,000
Other money	
Real estate (if you own a house or property)	
Other (e.g., jewellery, artwork)	
Total Assets (A)	$20,150
LIABILITIES	
Loans from pals or siblings	$80
Credit cards	
Line of credit	
Student loan	
Mortgage	
Car loan	
Other	
Total Liabilities (B)	$80
Net Worth (A – B)	$20,150 – $80
NET WORTH	$20,070

PART 3
Spend Your Money

What Money Skill Do You Need to Learn Next?

Now you know how to track your money and save it, but what happens if you spend too much and you can't hit your long- or short-term savings goals? You need a budget. Wait! Before you close the book and walk, just hear me out. I promise this doesn't have to be painful.

Sticking to a budget has many names. Sometimes it's called living within your means. Other times it's called minding your spending. It doesn't matter. They all mean the same thing: you don't spend as much as you make every time you get paid. That's it. The secret to financial success. And it's one of the five habits you need to start practising now.

Why Is Spending Your Money an Important Skill?

It's really just simple math. If you can't stick to your budget, you'll dip into your savings. Then your savings goals from Part 2 will never happen.

Spend too much and you're not saving. Sad but true. But you can turn it around.

How Will You Use This Skill in the Future?

Every! Single! Day! I think budgeting is the hardest part of all the money stuff we do whether we are young or old, rich or poor. If it were easy to stick to a budget, I wouldn't have a job, and you wouldn't be reading this book.

When you grow up, you'll have many more bills to pay and many more places you'll need to spend money. But the skill is the same. If you practise living within your means now (not spending as much as you make), you'll be in great shape when you start adulting.

What You Will Learn Throughout Part 3

- A simplified budget for life: I call it "knowing your Hard Limit"

- How to reduce spending in a way that doesn't feel icky

- How to borrow money when you don't have enough, and how to pay it back safely

- How credit cards can be scary and also helpful

The Easy, Simplified Budget for Life

Many people learn a basic budget in school these days. But I'm here to offer you a different way to "budget." Most times, the budget has a lot of categories and may look something like this when you're pretending to run a household:

Step 1: What is your income? (Part 1)

You have a job paying $63,000 a year in Ontario before tax. You use the online income tax calculator to see that your after-tax pay is $48,490 per year for the current year. Your answer may be slightly different depending on what year you are using when you calculate it, because tax rates change every year. Let's round to $48,000. Then, you divide by 12 months and get a take-home pay of $4,000 per month ($48,000/12 months).

Step 2: Add up monthly expenses.

MONTHLY INCOME	$4,000
MONTHLY EXPENSES	
Rent	$1,500
Utility bills	$300
Cellphone	$100
Internet	$100
Insurance payments	$80
Payments to debt (e.g., student loans, car loans)	$350 (car payment)
Subscriptions (e.g., streaming, apps)	$100 (Netflix, Crave, Disney+)
Gym membership	$50
Groceries	$800
Gas	$120
Shopping (e.g., clothing, gifts)	$50 ($600/year)
Transportation (e.g., taxi, transit)	
Entertainment (e.g., books, movies, concerts)	$100
Meals out	$50
Other	
TOTAL EXPENSES	$3,700
Surplus	$300

Step 3: What is the surplus (extra) or deficit (shortfall)?

Step 4: Outline what you can save or how much you need to reduce spending. In our example, $4,000 of income minus $3,700 of expenses means a surplus of $300 ($4,000 − $3,700). Therefore, in this example, you can save $300 a month!

This is a very good example of a solid budget. But let's take it one step further. I like to think of your monthly expenses in four categories.

Expense Categories

Fixed expenses: These are predictable and reoccurring. Things you have already promised to pay to someone else. For example, rent, cellphone bill, Netflix subscription.

Long-term savings: We've already covered this. Long-term savings is money you put aside to improve your future finances. For example, money for school or for your future nest egg.

Short-term savings: We've covered this too. Short-term savings is money you put aside to spend at a later date. For example, saving up to go on a trip.

Spending money: This is everything else. It's not a bill. It's not long-term savings. It's not short-term savings. It's your spending money. This is the money you can spend on whatever you want, as long as you have enough to eat and you're having fun. For example, lunch money, or money for entertainment like going to the movies or shopping for clothes or games.

When you're an adult, these categories will be the same, but with many more things in them. But hopefully, you'll be earning more money that you can both spend and save.

Simplified Budget

MONEY YOU CANNOT SPEND	MONEY YOU CAN SPEND
Fixed Expenses	Spending Money
Long-Term Savings	
Short-Term Savings	

The line between the money you cannot spend and the money you can spend is something I call your Hard Limit. It's the best and easiest budget in the world. Know your limit, and spend within it.

Let's do that example again, showing the four expense categories.

Step 2: Add Up Monthly Expenses

MONTHLY INCOME	$4,000
MONTHLY EXPENSES	
FIXED EXPENSES	
Rent	$1,500
Utility bills	$300
Cellphone	$100
Internet	$100
Insurance payments	$80
Payments to debt (e.g., student loans, car loans)	$350 (car payment)
Subscriptions (e.g., streaming, apps)	$100 (Netflix, Crave, Disney+)
Gym membership	$50
Total Fixed Expenses	$2,580
SAVINGS	
Total Long-Term Savings	$100
Total Short-Term Savings	$200
SPENDING MONEY	
Groceries	$800
Gas	$120
Shopping (e.g., clothing, gifts)	$50 ($600/year)
Transportation (e.g., taxi, transit)	
Entertainment (e.g., books, movies, concerts)	$100
Meals out	$50
Total Spending Money	$1,120
TOTAL EXPENSES	$4,000
Surplus	

MONEY YOU CANNOT SPEND: $2,880	MONEY YOU CAN SPEND: $1,120
Fixed Expenses: $2,580	Spending Money: $1,120
Long-Term Savings: $100	
Short-Term Savings: $200	

The most important detail in this example is that you're able to spend $1,120 each month however you choose for your day-to-day life. The Hard Limit for spending is $1,120. Know the limit. Spend within it.

This is a life skill. This is the key to budgeting when you're an adult, and you can start practising tomorrow!

9

David, Who Overspent

AGE:	14
SIBLING STATUS:	Has a younger brother
INCOME SOURCE(S):	Old enough to legally work but hasn't found a job; random jobs in the neighbourhood
REGULAR INCOME CALCULATION:	$200 in the next 4 weeks
CURRENT SAVINGS:	$0 in sock drawer

When we last met, David was determined to earn more and make drastic cuts to his spending so he would have enough money to buy a $500 video game console before the end of summer.

For the record, I told him at the time: "I think this plan is too tight. Maybe the 50–50 rule would be more realistic with a longer timeline to buy the console of three to four months."

He had shaken his head. "I know. But I think I can make this work."

We had decided then to connect in late July to see how things were going.

I met with David at the end of July. He was so happy when I greeted him at the door.

"Good news?" I asked.

"The best." He beamed. "I got the console."

"Wow!" I was so thrilled for him. "How did you do it so quickly?"

He looked sheepish and scrunched his face. "Uh . . ."

I cocked my head to the side. "What's up?"

"Well, I used my $20 and I borrowed money from my mom for it so I could get it faster."

"Whoa! Tell me about that."

"Like, three days after we met I got really bummed that I was going to have to wait for so long with summer so close."

"I get that. How did you approach her for it?" I was so curious. I've known his mom for years, and I was very surprised to hear that she would lend him money for video games.

"I took the projected income numbers that we made and showed them to her. I told her that all the money that I would have put toward savings would go to her instead."

"So, you rerouted the savings to pay back your mom."

"Yeah," he said excitedly. "And in that case, the $480 would be paid off by August 1st!"

"And that was it? She just said yes?"

He made it seem like it had been easy, but I was having a hard time believing that borrowing $480 from his mom had been that simple.

He shifted a bit uncomfortably. "I mean, yeah. She gave me the $480."

"And it's definitely a loan, right? Not a gift? When taking money from friends and family, you really need to be clear on that," I persisted.

"Definitely a loan and not a gift. She agreed to buy it now, but I have to pay her back the $60 a week until August 1st."

"Is she charging you interest?"

"Not unless I miss payments and go over the schedule."

"Okay. So it's interest-free as long as you pay the $60 a week. If you miss payments or fall behind, she will charge you interest."

"Yeah," he said, a bit less enthusiastically. "We signed a contract. It's on the fridge."

"That's good!" I said. "All personal loans should have a contract outlining the amount borrowed, when it's expected to be paid back, the interest, and what happens if payments are missed. This is the same when adults lend money to friends and family. Loans need a contract to make it clear as day and avoid arguments. And I like that it's on the fridge. Very direct."

"Yeah. I mark off the payment schedule every time I give her the $60. Like a countdown."

"I love that. No room for surprises."

"At first I thought it was really creative," he said.

"It was! Borrowing money can be tricky, though. Think about credit cards."

"Is borrowing money the same as 'debt' even though she's not charging interest yet?"

"Yep. You borrowed money, spent it, and now you have to make a minimum payment each week. That's debt."

I could see him squirm.

"It's okay. Borrowing money is a part of modern finances. Most people have mortgages* if they own a home, use lines of credit,* or have credit cards. Borrowing money safely is the only way to buy what you want before you have the savings. But you have to beware the payback schedule," I said with a smile.

"What's the payback schedule?"

"What you're agreeing to send them. How much, when, and for how long. If you have trouble meeting the payback schedule, it's usually a signal that you overspent."

"Well, then, I guess I may have," he said, and for the first time in all of our sessions, I felt tension in his voice.

"It's not going well?" I asked.

He let out a big, disappointed sigh. "No. Well, yes, I've made all my payments. I give her $60 cash on Fridays, but it's been so tight for me, and I'm worried about being able to do that ongoing. I don't know if I can afford to pay her the $60 weekly."

"That's interesting," I said.

"What is?"

"Well, the last time you were here, the amount you'd have to save in order to have the console by August 1st was the same, and you weren't worried about that being unrealistic. But now you're worried that paying the same amount of money to your mom is not realistic."

He raised his eyebrows. "That's true. That is weird."

"Why do you think that is?"

"I guess I felt like if I didn't save up, I'd only be letting myself down. But now that my mom has splurged on this for me, I know I'm letting her down, and there's a contract on the fridge. Like, accountability to someone else."

"I get that. That's debt. You have debt for the first time in your life, David. And debt can make people feel all kinds of things."

"The thing is, now that I have to pay this $60 each week, I'm always broke. I haven't hit the income goals I thought I would."

"Okay, so there are two things making this loan from Mom feel stressful, like you overspent. Thing one, your bills have just gone up because now you have a debt minimum payment of $60 every week. Thing two is that the income you projected to handle that repayment schedule is not panning out."

"There's one more thing," he said in a defeated tone.

"Lay it on me."

He let out a sigh. "Last week I was so short on spending money I had to borrow from my friend so I could still give my mom the $60. I borrowed 20 bucks from him. So, this week I have to pay $60 to my mom and $20 to my friend, and then I'll have nothing left."

"Did you make a payment schedule contract with your pal?"

He sort of smiled. "No, we don't do that. We borrow from each other a lot. Sometimes one of us is up and the others aren't. But I definitely want to pay him back within the month."

"I'm assuming it's interest-free?" I said, jokingly.

He laughed. "Yes. But I feel like I'm going to get stuck in a loop."

I nodded. "A debt loop. When you have to borrow from somewhere else to pay back someone you borrowed from already."

"Exactly. The payments I have to make to Mom reduce my spending money by so much that I have to borrow somewhere else until my income goes back up. Then I have to pay that person too."

"This is a really common problem. I work with plenty of adults who have borrowed too much and then get stuck in a debt loop. Paying off credit cards with lines of credit is the adult version of this."

"It sucks."

"It's not fun."

"So, what can I do?" he asked in a tone that made me sad. "I'm not really overspending. I'm just trying to hit the repayments to the debts I have."

"Technically, borrowing the $480 from your mom and buying the console before you had the money saved up *was* the overspending. You bought something you didn't have money for or the income to pay off timely."

"I guess you're right. I just thought I could pay it back."

"And you can. We are gonna make a plan. I'm actually really glad this happened."

He looked at me, brow furrowed. "What?"

"I'm not glad you're worried about money! But this is a really good lesson to learn about debt while you're young, with a parental loan."

He nodded. "I just want to pay it back and not have to ask her to extend the timeline."

"Let's see if you can." I opened up his Projected Future Income Calculation that we had calculated last time we met. "Last time you were here, you had $260 coming in during June and an estimated $300 coming in for July. How much of the $260 do you have left from June?"

"None. I gave my mom $60 four times, that's $240 paid off ($60 x 4), and then was short last week, so I had to borrow $20 from my friend."

"When does your pal want to be repaid?"

He scrunched up his face. "I mean, as soon as possible, but I've loaned him money in the past. I think he'd be okay to wait until I'm done paying Mom back. I just need to confirm with him."

"Alright, here's your debt map. The chart of everything you owe."

	AMOUNT OWING	WEEKLY MINIMUM PAYMENT
MOM LOAN	$240 left to repay ($480 – $240)	$60/week for four more weeks
FRIEND LOAN	$20	$0 once Mom loan paid off
TOTAL LIABILITIES	$260	$60

I sat forward. "Step 1, as you can probably guess, is to calculate what's coming in over the next four weeks to see if you can repay this." I showed him the Projected Future Income Calculation for July that we had done a month ago. "What didn't pan out or what doesn't feel realistic now?"

He looked at it. "I only have six lawn maintenance gigs. That's all I could book."

I changed it from 12 to six. "So your actual July income will be $240. Not $300."

He looked excited. "But that's great! That's what I owe my mom."

"But you also need some spending money, remember? That's how you ended up borrowing."

"Oh. Right." He looked me in the eye. "So, what's the least I could spend?"

David's Projected Future Income, Updated

Updated
July

Income Source	Random	Predictable	Reoccurring	Included in Regular Income	Tax Rate*	A Predictable Income amount $	B How many times in the next 4 weeks?	C Total Regular Income
Babysitting Olivia		X	Yes	No	$60/ month ($15 x 4 hours)	1	$60 ($60 x 1)
Tutoring		X	Yes	No	$25/ week	0	$0
Dog-walking Luna		X	Yes	No	$5/walk	12 (3 times/ week)	$60 ($5 x 12)
Babysitting Sammy	X		Yes	No	$15/ hour	4	$60 ($15 x 4)
Shovelling/ lawn mowing	X		Yes	No	$10/ house	6	$60 ($10 x 6)
Dog-walking Max	X		Yes	No	$10/ walk	0	$0 ($10 x 0)
TOTAL							$240

*Tax Rate from https://www.wealthsimple.com/en-ca/tool/tax-calculator/ontario

"Realistically? Let's find out." I turned to the keyboard again. "What are your expenses for July? I want to fill out a budget for you."

He looked at my chart. "Wow, I, like, don't spend anything on bills."

"You're young. But you've got a new bill. The minimum $60 per week to your mom. That's $240 a month ($60 x 4)."

"And I don't have any money for short- or long-term savings right now," he said.

I updated the chart. "What about spending money?"

"Lunches, movies, clothes? That kind of thing?" he asked.

"Exactly. Last time you were here you said that your normal income of $120 a month between babysitting Olivia and walking Luna is usually enough for you to get by."

"That's still right."

"That's $30 a week."

"Which I don't currently have."

"No. But you do have three levers to help you reach your goal. One, reduce spending. Two, earn more. And three, ask your mom for an extension. Spend less. Make more. Extend time. Those are your only options."

I could see him mulling it over.

"What if I only spend $5 on lunch, maybe three days a week?" he said.

I added $60 ($15 x 4) to meals out. "What else?"

He looked over the list. "I only pay for transit when I have money and in the wintertime. I bike everywhere right now, or my parents drive me. I don't have to buy gas. Or buy groceries."

"What about shopping and entertainment? Things like movies, books, concerts, games."

"That's where I spend, for sure. But, for the next four weeks, I could stop all spending on that stuff."

"Are you sure? It's summer. You'll probably want to do something."

"You're right. But I can keep it to, like, $40 a month. For sure. Maybe $10 a week or $20 for awesome stuff twice. And no shopping for July. Because I have these debts to pay and not enough income."

We filled out a simplified budget worksheet.

"You're still short."

"I see it."

"By $100."

"Shoot."

David's Simplified Budget Worksheet

MONTHLY INCOME	$240
MONTHLY EXPENSES	
FIXED EXPENSES	
Rent	
Utility bills	
Cellphone	
Internet	
Insurance payments	
Payments to debt (e.g., student loans, car loans)	$240 to Mom
Subscriptions (e.g., streaming, apps)	
Gym membership	
Total Fixed Expenses	$240
SAVINGS	
Total Long-Term Savings	$0
Total Short-Term Savings	$0
SPENDING MONEY	
Groceries	
Gas	
Shopping (e.g., clothing, gifts)	
Transportation (e.g., taxi, transit)	
Entertainment (e.g., books, movies, concerts)	$40
Meals out	$60
Total Spending Money	$100
TOTAL EXPENSES	$340
Surplus/Shortfall	–$100 ($240 – $340)

"What are the three levers again?" I counted them off on my fingers. "Spend less. Make more. Extend time. Can we do any of those here?"

"I can spend even less. Maybe lunch out only twice a week. That would save me $5 a week, saving $20 ($5 x 4 weeks) a month."

"Are you sure that's realistic?" I asked. "This is feeling a bit unsustainable."

"I can do it, I can do it."

I shrugged. "Okay." I made the change. "Anything else?"

He shook his head. "I think, given summer, I'll do stuff for entertainment. This is already feeling so tight. I can just make sure I eat at home or pack a lunch for things."

"Lever two. Make more?"

"Hmmm," he said. "I don't think I can earn more guaranteed money in July. It's possible, but I don't want to plan on it."

I nodded. "I agree. Well, if you reduce the meals out by $20 a month, your shortfall goes from $100 to $80. But it's still $80."

"What's lever three again?" David asked.

"Extend time. You could ask your mom if you can reduce the payments each week so that you break even, and it will take you longer to repay her."

"Ha. That's awkward."

"What is?" I asked.

"Well, I just couldn't wait for the console, but now I have to ask my mom to wait. Doesn't seem fair."

"This is what debt allows us to do. Have things that we shouldn't technically have yet because we can't actually afford it. Before credit cards were invented, you waited and saved up. It's a problem grownups also have. Not being able to wait. No delayed gratification. We all struggle with it from time to time."

"If I ask her for an extension, I'm worried she'll charge me interest."

David's Simplified Budget, Lever 1: Spend Less

MONTHLY INCOME	$240
MONTHLY EXPENSES	
FIXED EXPENSES	
Rent	
Utility Bills	
Cellphone	
Internet	
Insurance payments	
Payments to debt (e.g., student loans, car loans)	$240 to Mom
Subscriptions (e.g., streaming, apps)	
Gym membership	
Total Fixed Expenses	$240
SAVINGS	
Total Long-Term Savings	$0
Total Short-Term Savings	$0
SPENDING MONEY	
Groceries	
Gas	
Shopping (clothing, gifts, etc.)	
Transportation (e.g., taxi, transit)	
Entertainment (e.g., books, movies, concerts)	$40
Meals out	$40
Total Spending Money	$80
TOTAL EXPENSES	$320
Surplus/Shortfall	–$80

I nodded. "All you can do is ask. If she does, she does. Technically, this isn't a missed payment, but it is breaking the initial contract."

"How long do I have to ask my mom to wait?" he asked with a cringe.

"Let's math it out," I said. "Your shortfall is $80, which is $20 per week ($80/4 weeks)."

"So I ask her if I can give her $40 instead of $60 per week?"

"That would do it. It would give you the minimum spending money you need and allow you to pay her something."

"And then how much longer until I've repaid the $240 to her and the $20 to my friend?"

"For your mom, if you reduce the weekly payment from $60 per week to $40 per week, it will take you six weeks to pay it off ($240/$40 per week) instead of four."

"Okay, that's not as bad as I thought. Maybe she won't charge interest because it's only two weeks extra. Like, pay it off before school starts. And then I can just pay my friend back after that."

"If you think everyone will be cool with that, then it would work."

"I think so," he said and then made a face. "I hope so."

"Me too." I took a sip of water. "Do you have any other questions for today?"

"I guess I know what I'm supposed to put where, but my income comes in at random times. How do I stick to the budget when my money fluctuates so much?"

"Great question!" I said enthusiastically. "Managing a budget with self-employment income can be tricky."

I had a look at his projected July income.

"Since the money from babysitting Olivia and Sammy is $120 between them both, why don't you give all of that to your mom? Then, you'll only have to pay her $10 a week from the rest of the money."

He didn't say anything, but I could tell he was confused.

"You owe your mom $40 a week if she accepts these new loan terms, right?"

"Yes."

"That's $160 ($40 x 4 weeks) in July."

He nodded.

"Money from babysitting Olivia and Sammy only comes in once in the month. $60 each," I said.

"Yes."

"They aren't weekly paydays."

"No."

"So, if we earmark the $60 from Olivia and $60 from Sammy for your mom in July, then you will only owe her $40 for the rest of that month ($160 – $60 from Sammy – $60 from Olivia)."

"Oh, I see. Then, each week when I collect money from dog-walking and lawn stuff, I only give my mom $10 a week for four weeks to make up the $40 ($10 x 4 weeks)."

"Exactly. And you need $20 a week for $80 of monthly spending money ($80/4 weeks)."

"So whenever I get paid from Mrs. Rivere for walking Luna, the first $10 is for spending, and the rest I can't spend. It's for my mom."

"Yep."

He was working it out. "And any time I get paid for lawn stuff, the first $10 of that is also for spending money, and the rest I can't spend."

"Exactly! Your Hard Limit for spending is $80 per month, or $20 a week. You can't spend any more than that."

MONEY YOU CANNOT SPEND: $160	MONEY YOU CAN SPEND: $80
Fixed Expenses: $160 ($40 x 4)	Spending Money: $80
Long-Term Savings: $0	
Short-Term Savings: $0	

"Do you think it's realistic?" I asked.

"Definitely," he said. "The extension is key."

"If you can earn this money and stick to this budget, you'll have paid back everything to your mom by the end of the summer as long as she doesn't charge interest. Then you can pay your pal back, and after that, the monthly income that's normal for you can be spent, and you can save the rest."

"Save it up so that next time I don't end up in this mess again."

"That's right."

"What if she says no?" he asked. "Like, not even interest, what if she just says no?"

"Zero spending money for four weeks or interest and penalties."

"It's going to be tough if that's the case," he said.

"I can imagine. But also, imagine this as an adult when you can't just spend nothing because you have to buy food to eat, put gas in the car, and keep the lights on."

"That would be scary."

"It is. For many people. That's why it's important to use debt wisely and try not to overspend on it. It can get you into a pickle."

"I don't like debt," he said.

I smiled. "Debt isn't something to be scared of in life, just something that really needs to be planned properly and realistically before you take it on. I'm really happy you're getting this life lesson so early. Delayed gratification is a huge life skill that will benefit you in so many ways when you're grown-up."

"Can we meet up in September?" he asked. "Is that okay? I'd love to sit down once I've paid all this back."

I grinned at him. "I'd absolutely love that. Good luck! Have the best summer, and I hope you can negotiate the terms of the loan."

He started for the door out of the porch.

"Also, David!" I called. "Please tell your mom that I bought my raffle tickets for the neighbourhood party!"

He smiled a big toothy grin. "I will."

David was only 14 but had already found himself caught in a debt loop after overspending on the console and being unrealistic about how much money he would bring in. As a result, he had to reduce his spending and stick to a tight budget.

The more fixed expenses you have—the more bills—the less of your money you get to spend. Always pay attention to anything you agree to that increases your fixed expenses. Once you agree to a fixed expense, whether it's a loan, a credit card, rent, or a phone bill, you're on the hook for it. They get paid no matter what, and you have to live your life with what's left over.

CHAPTER 9 NITTY GRITTY

What Is a Mortgage?

- A mortgage is a big loan that someone uses to buy a house.

- For example, let's say the house is $500,000. If the person has $100,000 in savings to buy the house, they will have a $400,000 mortgage. They pay off this mortgage over a long period of time, usually 25 years. They are also charged interest.

- For more information, read https://www.canada.ca/en/financial -consumer-agency/services/mortgages/choose-mortgage.html /#toc0.

What Is a Line of Credit?

- A line of credit is a loan that lets you borrow money up to a specific maximum amount.

- You don't have to use all of it. You can use as much or as little as you need.

- You only pay interest on the amount you borrowed. For example, if you had a line of credit that allowed you to borrow up to $5,000 but you only borrowed $2,000, you'd pay interest on the $2,000, not the $5,000.

- The interest rate is usually variable on a line of credit and lower than a credit card.

- Read more here: https://www.canada.ca/en/financial-consumer -agency/services/loans/loans-lines-credit.html.

Do You Know Your Stuff?

Test your knowledge with these True or False questions.

QUESTION 1: A gift is when someone gives you money that you pay back interest-free over a long period of time.

False. A gift never has to be repaid.

QUESTION 2: The payback schedule is what you're agreeing to send them: how much, when, and for how long. *True.*

QUESTION 3: If you have trouble meeting the payback schedule, it's usually a signal that you overspent. *True.*

QUESTION 4: A debt loop is when you have to borrow from somewhere else to repay someone you borrowed from already. *True.*

QUESTION 5: All debt is bad.

False! Borrowing money is a part of modern life. You just have to make sure you can handle the payment schedule and pay it back without ending up in a debt loop.

HOMEWORK

Step 1: Fill out the simplified budget form for yourself.

Simplified Budget Worksheet

MONTHLY INCOME (Use the Regular Income Calculator, p. 20, to determine this.)	
MONTHLY EXPENSES	
FIXED EXPENSES	
Rent	
Utility bills	
Cellphone	
Internet	
Insurance payments	
Payments to debt (e.g., student loans, car loans)	
Subscriptions (e.g., streaming, apps)	
Gym membership	
Total Fixed Expenses	
SAVINGS	
Total Long-Term Savings	
Total Short-Term Savings	
SPENDING MONEY	
Groceries	
Gas	
Shopping (e.g., clothing, gifts)	

SPENDING MONEY CONTINUED	
Transportation (e.g., taxi, transit)	
Entertainment (e.g., books, movies, concerts)	
Meals out	
Total Spending Money	
TOTAL EXPENSES	
Surplus/Shortfall	

STEP 2: Decrease any expenses you can so that you have no shortfall.

STEP 3: Increase savings if there is a surplus.

STEP 4: Calculate your Hard Limit for spending.

MONEY YOU CANNOT SPEND	MONEY YOU CAN SPEND: HARD LIMIT
Fixed Expenses:	Spending Money:
Long-Term Savings:	
Short-Term Savings:	

10

Tania, Who Just Needed Money for Life

AGE:	18
SIBLING STATUS:	Has a younger brother
INCOME SOURCE:	Part-time job at the local arena
REGULAR INCOME CALCULATION:	$2,248 in the next 4 weeks
CURRENT SAVINGS:	$2,500 in savings account; $2,136 in a TFSA
SAVINGS GOALS:	Post-secondary school and a grad trip/trip to see her grandmother

After our last meeting, Tania went out to start saving money for the trip and for school, and her intention was to have no spending money. We had planned to meet again in late July after her trip, but she reached out to me to check in at the end of June, just before Phase 2 of our plan was supposed to start. We met just before the trip was supposed to happen. The meeting got off to a bumpy start.

"Hey, Tania!" I said when she appeared onscreen.

"Hi," she said flatly.

I could tell she was not happy. I had a feeling that would be the case before the meeting. She had reached out a few weeks ago and asked if we could do our follow-up meeting before the trip.

"How's it going?" I asked.

She bit her bottom lip and looked away from the screen. She was sort of bouncing a bit. I suspected she was moving her foot up and down quickly below her desk. She was definitely agitated and upset. She took a while to speak because I think she was trying not to cry.

"Are you okay, Tania?" I asked gently.

She shook her head no, but didn't speak.

"Want to take a minute?"

She nodded.

"I'm going to go get a glass of water," I said. "I'll be back in a minute or so."

She nodded again, her screen went black, and she muted herself. I left my screen on but just stood beside the computer. I didn't go get water. After a few minutes her screen came back on, and she unmuted herself.

She cleared her throat. "Sorry about that."

"Don't be. I don't know exactly why you're here before our originally scheduled meeting in July, but I imagine it's because the plan to spend zero money didn't work out the way you hoped."

"It didn't."

Oof. I felt for her. "I'm sorry that happened. It's really hard to fail at our financial plans. It can make us feel hopeless."

She quickly wiped away an escaped tear and shook her head. "Don't be sorry. It's not your fault. It's just impossible to do the right thing financially."

I tilted my head to the side. "What's the right thing? Financially?"

"Save money. Don't go into debt."

"Those are good pillars, but it's much more complicated."

"It shouldn't be. You spend less than you make, you save it, and you don't buy things unless you have the money."

"You think that's impossible," I said, my voice full of empathy.

"I know it is. For me. Not for rich people, or people with rich parents. But for me, it's impossible. I work so hard. I spend so little. Constantly saying no. Always going without. No fun. And I save, save, save, and no matter how hard I try, I keep having to dip into my savings." Her voice started shaking. "And now I don't have enough saved to see my grandmother. I can't go on the trip, and no matter what I do in the next six months, I won't have enough." Tears fell.

"Oh, Tania, that's really hard," I said. "Are you sure there's no way to go? Maybe we can find a solution."

"Ugh, I'm just so over it. I've been trying not to spend any money and tracking any spending I did with my budgeting app, and no matter what I do, there's no way to do this."

"How much do you have saved right now?"

She slumped. "For the trip, I only have the $2,500 saved. The $2,500 I already had. I spent all the money I was supposed to put aside for the trip. On payday, I'd get the $190, then put $33.25 to bills, and $67.83 to the trip fund, and $89 to the school fund. I even opened a Tax-Free Savings Account (TFSA) when I turned 18 for the school savings and had the $89 automatically come out each week on payday to that account. But so many things went wrong in the last few months."

"What happened?"

"My laptop broke, so I had to repair it and it cost $300. Two of my friends had birthdays and we all went to get our nails done and go out for lunch. It came up to $100 because we also covered theirs. Things like that." She let out a big sigh and sounded so defeated. "I just needed money for life."

"That's normal. Spending nothing was unrealistic."

"I thought I would try and spend nothing and maybe actually spend like $20 a week or something and save the rest. But I ended up spending so much more. Closer to $40 a week." She put her face in her hands.

"Are you upset that you couldn't stick to the plan, or that you think you can't go on the trip?"

"The trip," she said softly. "I really want to go. I want to see my grandmother. I want to be with my friends before we all go away for university. I can't believe I spent the money. This trip is so important to me. How was it not enough to make me save?"

"Tania, I think you can still go on the trip."

"What? How?" She looked at me, confused. "It's next week. I'd have to book flights, like, tonight and pay for almost all of it this week. It's going to cost $5,000 all in. I don't have $5,000. Not even close."

"What about the TFSA? The $89 per week you've been saving for 24 weeks. That's $2,136 ($89 x 24 weeks)!"

She looked indignant. "What? That's school money."

"I know, but it's also money you saved up. You have a year to save for school."

She put her hands up. "No. No. I'm not comfortable with that."

"What is making you feel uncomfortable?" I asked.

"I don't think I could enjoy the trip if I used money that was supposed to keep me out of debt when I'm in school."

I nodded. "I get that."

"See? I can't go," she said. "Unless I used a credit card."

"Did you apply for one?"

"My aunt co-signed one. She said I should have a credit card now that I'm 18. For my own financial independence." She looked nervous. "Is that bad?"

"That actually can be very helpful," I said reassuringly. "Having a credit card will start to build your credit score. For better or worse."

"How?"

"This is a major topic, but your credit score* is a score, between 300 and 850, that represents how well you manage debt on your credit report.* Future creditors will use it when deciding whether or not you're a good risk. For example, if you apply for a loan in the future, the lender, the bank, can look at your credit score and see the history of how you manage debt. Are you a person who misses payments? Do you max out your cards every month and carry big balances? The lower your score, the less likely you'll be able to get good loans or interest rates in the future."

"That all seems like after-university stuff, though."

"Yes and no. A lot of landlords will ask for a credit score. So when you move out—"

She interrupted. "Ha. If I can afford to."

"Well, hopefully all the schooling will lead to a job that pays you enough to move out," I said with a smile. "But no matter what, building a solid credit score while you're young is great. Plus, you get the experience of using a credit card, getting all the perks as long as you don't overspend and get into trouble with it."

"There are perks to a credit card? I thought they were evil."

"They can be. Credit cards are like your best pal or your worst enemy in one. Like a frenemy."

"I know they are bad because they charge interest, but I don't really understand that fully."

"Credit cards can harm in three ways: they can get you in debt from overspending, they charge high interest when you can't pay it back, and they can hurt your credit score when used incorrectly."

"How can it get me into debt?"

"Well, it's extremely easy to spend money you don't have using a credit card. I'm sure you've seen people pay for things at the store, and they don't even have to put in a code most times. Just tap the card and it's done. Same on the internet. Once you put your credit card into online stores, you don't need to think before you spend. That's how it gets people into trouble. They accidentally overspend and then can't pay it off. It's too easy."

She looked uncomfortable. "Why can't they pay it off?"

"So many different reasons. But the main thing that's the same with everyone is that as soon as you borrow money to spend on something, you have to pay it back. Plus, you still have to pay for your regular life. Plus, if you miss the grace period, you have to pay it back with interest. Interest is an amount of money you owe on top of the amount you borrowed."

"I'm confused."

"This is an overly simplified example, but it helps to get the point across. Let's say you go shopping and spend $100, and you don't pay it off that month. If the credit card charges 25% interest per month, you'd have to pay $25 in interest ($100 x 25% = $25). So now you'd owe $125, which is the original amount you spent plus the extra interest."

She nodded. "So, the interest makes it more expensive."

"Exactly. And if you're buying something on a credit card, you probably don't have cash just sitting around. Then you can't pay it off, you have to borrow more to pay for daily life, and then your credit score gets hurt. It can start a cycle called a debt loop. Which is not good."

"Why don't I just cut this card up and never use it?"

"One of the main benefits of having a credit card is that as long as you pay it off within the time period they allow, called the grace period, there is no interest charged! You can use it and pay it off without being charged any interest."

"So, it's free—until you're late?" she asked.

"Yes. Plus, using it and paying it off on time is what helps to build up your credit score. And depending on your card, you may even be able to collect points that you can use for other things like travel, cash back, that kind of thing."

"Okay, I think I get it. As long as I use it and can pay it off, I won't be charged interest and I'll get the benefits."

"Exactly. But you have to have a plan to pay it back. You don't want to accidentally overspend and get yourself into debt that you can't get out of."

She nodded. "I don't think I should use this for my trip. It scares me."

"You don't have to be scared. If you can realistically handle the repayment schedule, it's not overspending. You have to have a plan. Let's math out a budget, a realistic one, to see how long it would take you to pay it back and if you can swing it."

She nodded but didn't say anything. I could tell she was mulling it over.

I shared my screen and pulled up a spreadsheet.

Tania's Total Savings

SHORT-TERM SAVINGS	$2,500
LONG-TERM SAVINGS (TFSA)	$2,136 ($89 x 24 weeks)
TOTAL TRIP COST	$5,000
SHORTFALL	–$364 (rounded to $365)

"Tania, I think it's okay to use the money in the TFSA for this big trip, to save the interest on the credit card, and to go on this important trip."

"Isn't it irresponsible?" she asked gloomily.

"You're young, you have a job, and you're saving so much so you can avoid student loans. You have worked so hard!"

"But last time we calculated everything out, we figured I would almost break even for school, only a $1,280 surplus. If I use this money for the trip, I'm short $3,720 ($5000 – $1280). That will end up on a credit card or student loan at some point."

I let out a big breath. "Maybe that's true. It's hard to know. So much can happen in the next four years for you. Maybe you'll be able to work more than one shift a week during school. Maybe the costs won't be as high. Or maybe you'll have to take out a $3,700 student loan in your last year of school. We don't know for sure. But $365 on a credit card for a month is not going to make or break your ability to pay for school or throw you into debt for the rest of your life. It will, however, absolutely make or break your ability to go on this once-in-a-lifetime trip. It's not like you're pulling the money out to buy something meaningless, and it's not so much money that you can't pay it off. This matters."

She nodded again.

"Tell you what. Let's make a budget to see how long it would take you to catch up. To go on the trip and then pay back the money you borrowed from the long-term savings. Obviously, spending no money wasn't possible, but how much could you spend and still save that money? Then, you can make an informed decision!"

She sat up straighter. "That sounds good."

"Awesome." I cheered. "At our last meeting, we projected that Future Income will go to $2,248 when you get home from the trip because you'll have full-time hours."

"Yeah, but I have to save that money for school. Like we already talked about, I need to save $1,830, and now I'll have to pay this back as well."

I nodded. "Right. And my affordability rule of thumb is that you are not allowed to buy something on credit that you can't reasonably pay off in three months."

"How do I know?" she asked as she wrote down my last point.

"Let's make a budget." I shared my budget template with her and filled it out as we went. "I know you pay $100 for your phone each month, and your gym membership is $18 a month, and I know that you pay for a streaming app that's $15."

"I also pay for some groceries and toiletries, plus spending money and transit."

"Totally, but let's fill out your fixed expenses first."

"Those are fixed. I pay for those things every month."

"I understand. I'm not saying they are optional, but I'm trying to calculate the bills you pay each month that are predictable and reoccurring. Like the gym membership, it's $18 every month. Same with your subscriptions and phone bill. Groceries and toiletries or clothes fluctuate. One month maybe $40, the next $30."

"I see. It's not about importance but, like, how the expense happens."

"Right. Fixed expenses mean all the money you cannot spend each month because it's already promised to someone else."

She looked at the chart. "I think that's it for bills."

"I'm not adding a $17 minimum payment you'd have to make on the $365."

"Is that because I'd pay it off within the grace period?"

"Yes. The minimum payment on a loan or a credit card is the amount you must pay. You have to, no choice. Can't get out of it. So it's a fixed expense. The amount you put on the loan or credit card that's more than the minimum is actually a form of long-term savings!"

"Because it's bettering my future finances and it's a choice."

"You got it," I said, smiling.

"And debt increases your cost of living because of the interest that you have to pay each month," she said. "And the interest is part of the minimum payment, right?"

I nodded. "If the interest rate is 25%, you're paying approximately $7 in interest on the $365 and $10 to principal. The principal is the actual amount of debt you have." I turned back to the chart. "What were some of the things you needed to spend money on that you think will continue in the future?"

"I always end up spending money on groceries or toiletries. My parents don't buy the right hair products for my curly hair. It's expensive. I also like certain groceries they don't want to buy. So I usually spend $80 a month at the grocery store since food and toiletries are so expensive."

I wrote that in. "What about entertainment? Going out? Getting a meal with friends?"

She shook her head. "I try to say no to almost everything, but I do love books. I'll usually spend $40 a month on books or records, and I'll go out for dinner with friends maybe once or twice. It's usually $25 no matter what I do. Eat a meal out, go to a movie, go bowling—whatever. It's $50 a month to go out. This is why I couldn't spend nothing."

I nodded. "I know. It's so hard." I turned back to the chart. "What about the other categories—clothes, shopping, transit?"

"My transit is around $85 for the month."

I put the expenses into Tania's budget. "What about clothes, shoes, that kind of thing?"

"Hardly anything. I usually try to save $30 a month so I can buy something when I need it. Like a sweater, shoes . . ." Her voice lowered and she hung her head. "I really thought I could do the library thing, the potluck-dinner-with-friends thing, and not buy anything for six months, but I couldn't. I don't have an extravagant life. I feel like I'm so careful, but everything is still so expensive."

"It may not be as bleak as you think." I tallied everything up. "Let's look at the savings goals we made last time."

I pulled it up on the screen.

"Phase 1 is over. Now you're about to start into full-time work in Phase 2. The goal is to put aside $1,830 for long-term savings when you start earning $2,248 a month."

I showed her the budget forecast.

"When you start working full-time this summer, your projected expenses will be $418 a month. Still about $5,016 a year ($418 x 12

Tania's Budget for Phase 2, Full-Time

MONTHLY INCOME	$2,248 ($14.05 x 40 hours x 4 weeks)
MONTHLY EXPENSES	
FIXED EXPENSES	
Rent	
Utility bills	
Cellphone	$100
Internet	
Insurance payments	
Payments to debt (e.g., student loans, car loans)	$0 (unless she misses a payment)
Subscriptions (e.g., streaming, apps)	$15
Gym membership	$18
Total Fixed Expenses	$133
SAVINGS	
Total Long-Term Savings	$1,830 (from Phase 2, how much to save for school)
Total Short-Term Savings	$0
SPENDING MONEY	
Groceries	$80
Gas	
Shopping (e.g., clothing, gifts)	$30
Transportation (e.g., taxi, transit)	$85
Entertainment (e.g., books, movies, concerts)	$40
Meals out	$50
Total Spending Money	$285
TOTAL EXPENSES	$418 ($285 + $133)
Surplus/Shortfall	$0

months). That's good. Almost exactly the same as our projections from before."

"So, what do I need to do?"

"The way I see it, next month, July, you'll go on the trip. You'll put approximately $365 onto the credit card for your trip, and pay it off within the grace period before you're charged interest."

"And I use the money from my long-term savings too?"

"Correct. But you can save it all back. You have 14 months before the start of school next year to pay back the $365 to long-term savings. Over 14 months, that's approximately $26 a month ($365/14). So, you'll increase your savings from $1,830 to $1,856 and reduce your spending from $418 to $392 per month."

She nodded. "Okay, but what about the other money I took from the TFSA? The $2,136. What would it be like if I made myself totally whole again?"

I scrunched my face up. "Right. Well, the budget will have to reduce more," I said. "Let's see how much more and then you can decide if the trip is worth it."

I started calculating.

"Taking $2,136 from the TFSA plus putting $365 on the credit card in July is a total of $2,501. You need to replace that savings over 14 months. That's a little over $178 per month ($2,501/14). That means you'd have to reduce your spending money from $418 to about $240. ($418 – $178.38)"

I frowned. "I think that's unrealistic. Look at your budget. Your bills alone are $133, and then you'd only be left with $107 ($240 – $133). You already saw that it's unrealistic to spend nothing."

She looked devastated. "So, I can't go see my grandma because I can't afford it." I think she was about to cry. I scanned the screen, desperate to find another solution.

"Okay!" I said. "What if we increase the savings over the entire time you're in school! Like, you don't need to save it all before you go."

Spend less.

Earn more.

Extend time.

"What do you mean?"

I smiled. "There are 62 months from your trip to your university graduation: 14 months before school, then 12 months each year that you're in it (12 months x 4 years = 48 months). Repaying $2,501 over 62 months (14 + 48) means a reduction of spending by only $40 a month ($2,501/62) once you're home from your trip!"

A massive smile broke over her face.

"Yes. Okay. Like, I can reduce meals out to $30 a month from $50, saving $20, and reduce transit by not taking taxis, saving another $20. That's it. That's $40 right there, but I can still take transit, buy stuff, go out at least once a month."

I looked at her budget. "If your fixed expenses are $133 and we reduce your spending money by $40 per month from $285 to $245, total monthly spending is $378, instead of $418."

She nodded.

"So, total annual spending would be $4,536 ($378 x 12 months), not your original $5,016 per year."

"That feels really doable."

"Right?" I said, already happy for her. I clapped my hands. "I feel like you're excited."

"I am! That feels realistic. Also, it's one extra shift per month at my job when I'm in university. So if I don't want to reduce spending when I get there, I can work one or two days a week and make even more."

"I'm so glad. I feel like you were really stressing, and I'm so glad we could find a way that you can say yes to the trip. I know it's really important to you."

Tania's Reduced Budget, Updated for New Savings

SPENDING MONEY	
Groceries/Toiletries	$80
Gas	
Shopping (e.g., clothing, gifts)	$30
Transportation (e.g., taxi, transit)	$65
Entertainment (e.g., books, movies, concerts)	$40
Meals out/going out	$30
TOTAL SPENDING MONEY	$245
TOTAL EXPENSES	$378 ($245 + $133)
Surplus/Shortfall	$0

She started to tear up again and just nodded. I took a big breath, relieved.

"Here is your updated budget and savings table with annual spending reduced to $4,536."

She sat forward. "So, assuming I only work 48 weeks a year because of holidays and vacation, every time I get paid my $562 per week, I put $61.25 ($245/4) into my chequing account to be spent, I put $467.50 ($1,870/4) into long-term savings, and $33.25 ($133/4) goes toward my bills."

"Yes. I mean, again, you could round it," I offered. "Put $60 to spending, $35 to bills, $467 to savings."

She thought for a moment, then giggled. "No . . . I really love the specifics. Every penny counts!"

We laughed.

"So? How do you feel?" I asked. "On this budget, you are within $2,585 (original $1,280 surplus + $1,305 new debt) of where you were originally supposed to be, but you went on the trip!"

Tania's Updated Budget and Savings

	LONG-TERM SAVINGS	SCHOOL EXPENSES	SPENDING MONEY	LONG-TERM SAVINGS BALANCE
PHASE 1: PART-TIME BEFORE SCHOOL	~~To save Jan–June (Phase 1) $89 x 24 weeks~~			~~$2,136~~
PHASE 2: JULY	$1,870 – $365 = $1,505			$1,505
PHASE 2: FULL-TIME BEFORE SCHOOL	$1,870/month for 13 months			$24,310
YEAR 1	+$10,256 (from income)	–$12,500	–$4,536	$19,035
YEAR 2	+$10,256 (from income)	–$12,500	–$4,536	$12,255
YEAR 3	+$10,256 (from income	–$12,500	–$4,536	$5,475
YEAR 4	+$10,256 (from income)	–$12,500	–$4,536	–$1,305

Tania put her hand on her chest and let out a big breath. "I'm so relieved. I'm so happy I can go!"

"Yes, yes!" I said. "Book the trip now. Like, get off this call and do it right away!"

"Thank you. Thank you so much."

I was so relieved. She had worked so hard, and I really wanted her to be able to enjoy this trip. Money is a tool that we use to keep ourselves financially safe, but also to experience life. I couldn't wait to hear about the trip when we met next time.

Tania's Simplified Budget Worksheet, Updated

MONTHLY INCOME	$2,248 ($14.05 x 40 hours x 4 weeks)
MONTHLY EXPENSES	
FIXED EXPENSES	
Rent	
Utility bills	
Cellphone	$100
Internet	
Insurance payments	
Payments to debt (e.g., student loans, car loans)	$0 (unless she misses a payment)
Subscriptions (e.g., streaming, apps)	$15
Gym membership	$18
Total Fixed Expenses	$133
SAVINGS	
Total Long-Term Savings	$1,870
Total Short-Term Savings	$0
SPENDING MONEY	
Groceries	$80
Gas	
Shopping (e.g., clothing, gifts)	$30
Transportation (e.g., taxi, transit)	$65
Entertainment (e.g., books, movies, concerts)	$40
Meals out	$30
Total Spending Money	$245
TOTAL EXPENSES	$378 ($245 + $133)
Surplus/Shortfall	$0

MONEY YOU CANNOT SPEND: $2,003	MONEY YOU CAN SPEND: $245 HARD LIMIT
Fixed Expenses: $133	Spending Money: $245
Long-Term Savings: $1,870	
Short-Term Savings: $0	

CHAPTER 10 NITTY GRITTY

What Is Your Credit Report?

- Your credit report is a summary of all the money you've borrowed, known as your credit history.

- It starts when you're 18.

- It has your credit score on it. This is a three-digit number between 300 and 850 based on a formula that shows how well you managed credit in the past.

- For more information, read here: https://www.canada.ca/en /financial-consumer-agency/services/credit-reports-score.html.

Do You Know Your Stuff?

Test your knowledge with these True or False questions.

QUESTION 1: It's good to delay having a credit card as long as you can.

False. If you never have a credit card, you can't start your credit score. Having a credit card early will start to build your credit score.

QUESTION 2: Your credit score is a score, 300–850, where 300 is low, and 850 is great. *True.*

QUESTION 3: The grace period is the period of time you have to pay off a credit card without being charged interest. *True.*

QUESTION 4: Fixed expenses are things that are not optional, like groceries.

False. A fixed expense is money you can't spend each month because it's already promised to someone else. Typically, it's predictable and recurring.

QUESTION 5: The three levers to hit your goals are spend less, earn more, and extend time. *True.*

HOMEWORK

Using the Simplified Budget Worksheet below, including the income and expenses provided, calculate the following: a student needs to have $2,400 in two years (24 months) and saves $100 a month to long-term savings.

Calculating the Levers

1. **SPEND LESS.** If the student reduced spending by $20 per month and saved it, how much would they have in 24 months?

ANSWER:

Simplified Budget Worksheet

MONTHLY INCOME:	$515
MONTHLY EXPENSES	
FIXED EXPENSES	
Rent	
Utility bills	
Cellphone	$80
Internet	
Insurance payments	
Payments to debt (e.g., student loans, car loans)	$0
Subscriptions (e.g., streaming, apps)	$20
Gym membership	$0
Total Fixed Expenses	$100
SAVINGS	
Total Long-Term Savings	$100
Total Short-Term Savings	$0
SPENDING MONEY	
Groceries	$60
Gas	
Shopping (e.g., clothing, gifts)	$50
Transportation (e.g., taxi, transit)	$65
Entertainment (e.g., books, movies, concerts)	$80
Meals out	$60
Total Spending Money	$315
TOTAL EXPENSES	$515 ($315 + $100 + $100)
Surplus/Shortfall	$0

(24 months x $100 existing monthly savings) + (24 months x $20 of NEW monthly savings) = $2,880

EXISTING SAVINGS	$100 x 24 months = $2,400
NEW SAVINGS	$20 x 24 months = $480
TOTAL SAVINGS	$2,400 + $480 = $2,880

2. EARN MORE: If the student earned $10 more a month and saved it, how much would they have in 24 months?

ANSWER:

EXISTING SAVINGS	$100 x 24 months = $2,400
NEW SAVINGS	$10 x 24 months = $240
TOTAL SAVINGS	($2,400 + $240) = $2,640

(24 months x $100 existing monthly savings) + (24 months x $10 of NEW monthly savings) = $2,640

3. EXTEND TIME: How much more could they spend per month if they extended the time to save from 24 months to four years (48 months)?

ANSWER:

$2,400/48 months = $50 a month would have to go to long-term savings (instead of $100). Reducing the amount from $100 to $50 means $50 of extra spending a month ($100 – $50).

11

Mia, the Big Spender

AGE:	13
SIBLING STATUS:	Middle kid between two sisters
INCOME SOURCE:	Has a regular allowance
REGULAR INCOME CALCULATION:	$100 in the next 4 weeks
CURRENT SAVINGS:	$20

When I sat down with Mia and her mother for our next meeting, it was the first time I had ever seen Mia with a frown on her face. Sofia also looked unimpressed. It was June. They were in my office a week before grade 8 grad.

"Hey, everyone," I said, hoping to lighten the mood.

"Hi, Shannon," Sofia said in a tone that made me feel like Mia was in trouble.

"So, I'm assuming things are not where we'd hoped?" I offered.

Mia just looked at the table, almost a bit embarrassed.

"She spent it all," Sofia said.

Mia piped up. "Not all of it."

I could tell they were in an argument. "Want to tell me what happened?" I asked.

Sofia didn't say anything, but nodded her head at Mia as if to say, "You go. You tell."

Mia let out a long breath. "I only have $20 saved," she said gloomily and didn't look at me.

"Over the whole four months!" Sofia interrupted. "Every week, she'd move money from the savings bucket to the spending. I saw it on the app and I didn't say anything! Because I knew she needed to learn this lesson for herself. She—"

Mia winced.

I held up my hand. "Hold on a sec, Sofia."

"Sorry," she said and sat back in her chair.

"Don't be. I just want to give Mia a minute here. These things happen and they aren't easy."

Sofia folded her arms across her chest.

"Mom," Mia said softly. "Can you go in the waiting room?"

Sofia lifted an eyebrow and looked from Mia to me. I didn't say anything. She sighed.

"Okay, Miss." She kissed Mia on the head. "I hope you listen to Shannon this time."

I got up to open the door. Sofia gave me a big hug and then went to sit outside.

"Hey, Mia," I said, sitting back down.

Her eyes were watery. "Hey."

I handed her a box of tissues. "Tell me what happened."

"I did listen," she started. "I tried. I did all the things we planned."

"And?"

"I just couldn't stick to it. I set it up, but I didn't follow through."

"This is the reason I have a job," I said, hoping a joke would make her laugh. "Grown-ups are the same."

She sniffed and smiled. "I can't get the dress. Grad is next week. I have to wear one of my sister's old ones."

I sighed. "That's hard, buddy. I'm sorry."

She shrugged. "My fault."

Oof. I felt for her. "Where did the plan go off the rails?" I asked.

She let out a big breath. "Well, it started out really great."

"Tell me about it."

"My mom would only deposit the $20 into it each Friday. She kept the $5 and any bonus money back for savings."

"This all sounds great. But I know it didn't work out, so when did things go wrong?"

She rolled her eyes. "Like, the first week."

"How?"

"Well, I have one of those debit cards that you can tap to purchase. Do you know what I'm talking about?"

Yikes. I did. "I do. It's called contactless payment. It's very convenient. But it makes budgeting extremely hard. I see this a lot."

"Try impossible! I don't even realize when I am spending money. I ran out the first week by Tuesday!"

"Do you know what you were spending on?" I ventured.

"Yes. This account automatically has a spending tracking app."

"That is cool!"

She laughed. "Yeah, now I can see all the stupid places I spent money."

"Hey, hey," I said. "Go easy on yourself. I'm sure the places you spent money meant something at the time."

She shook her head. "Not really. When I go back and look, it's all on stuff that I'm not really happy about."

"Like what?"

"Like, endless cafés, lunches out, clothes, and makeup."

"Weren't those the same expenses as before, though?"

"Yes, for sure, but I kept running out of money mid-week and then I'd move money from savings to spending."

"I see."

"Yeah." She shook her head in exasperation. "And she let me! Why, Shannon, why?"

I chuckled. "I think maybe she didn't want to be the bad guy?"

"Well, I wish she had been. I have nothing saved. After four months and many bonus chores. Every time I'd overspend and take the money back from her, I'd vow that I'd do way more bonus chores to make it back and spend way less the next week."

"Then what would happen?"

"I'd start the weekend off being like, 'I can't go to cafés at all. I can't go out for lunch. No shopping. No books or movies.' Then Sunday or Monday would roll around and we'd go to the mall at lunchtime, and I felt so mad that I was so broke I'd just be like, 'Whatever I don't care, I'll do another bonus chore.' And I'd tap my card and boom. It was gone. On expensive drinks and cheap T-shirts."

"Do you regret the purchases?"

"Big time," she said.

"Unhappy spending," I said.

"What's that?"

"It's a term I coined a long time ago to represent money that we have spent on something or an experience that we regret later."

"But if I have no savings, aren't all my expenses regrets? Like, I shouldn't have spent anything, right?"

"Not at all! You had $20 a week to spend on whatever you wanted. That money was supposed to be spent! You don't need to feel bad about using it. But when we are trying to save, maybe we are trying to reduce our expenses, and we can't buy everything we want because we will overspend."

"Tell me about it," she joked.

"So, the idea of happy or unhappy spending came from the fact that we only have so much spending money each month. All of us, adults too, have to make choices so that we don't overspend. When there's only so much money, you want to make sure that the things you do spend money on make you happy."

She thought about this for a moment. "Make it count."

"Exactly! So, let's figure out your happy and unhappy spending."

"Okay!"

She was excited as she pulled out the app that had tracked her expenses over the last four months. She frowned when she looked at it. "It's, like, the same five or six places over and over."

She wasn't wrong: cafés, movie theatre, cheap accessories, expensive makeup, transit, grocery store.

She shook her head. "Frappuccinos, movies, shirts, makeup, getting around, and food." She threw her hands up. "My life."

I smiled. "Nothing wrong with that."

"Sure, if I could afford it on $20 a week."

"Let's take a look at the last month of expenses. Can you rate each expense out of five for emotional return on investment?"

She scrunched up her face, confused. "Huh?"

I smiled. "Emotional return on investment. EROI. How happy did something make you when you bought it? Five out of five (5/5) would be so happy. No regrets, even now. A one out of five (1/5) would be unhappy. Maybe happy in the moment, but now when you look back, you wish you hadn't done it."

"You mean which ones do I regret? The ones I wish I didn't do?"

"Yes." I pointed at the café transactions. "How about Frappuccinos?"

She thought. "Two out of five (2/5)."

"Wow! That's not high. So Frappuccinos are low on the happiness?"

"I love going for coffee with my pals, but I can get tea for $2. I don't have to get a $6 drink every time. I regret those big time. It's the kind of thing that as soon as it's done, I'm like, 'Ugh, why did I do that?'"

"Noted," I said and wrote it down. "What about movies?"

"Five out of five (5/5)," she said right away.

"You like the movies."

She smiled. "I love them, plus it's the only thing we do on the weekends and I would be so sad to miss them. It's one of the main reasons I kept having to ask Mom for money."

"What do you mean?"

"I overspent on weekends. I'd buy stuff I shouldn't buy and I never want to miss the movies on the weekend. I'd overspend and then ask my mom for my savings or do a bonus chore and get money for it right away. I'd run out of money by Tuesday."

"Gotcha." I wrote down 5/5 for movies. "Clothes and makeup?"

She waffled on this. "Maybe a three? No, a four. No, a three. Hmmm, I don't know."

"What's making it tough to decide?"

"I love clothes and makeup. So I want to say even a five out of five (5/5), but I just overdid it. Something about being able to just tap my card. When I used to bring cash into the store, I was really aware that I didn't want to spend more than $10, but with the debit card that I could tap, I didn't have to be so careful. I just overdid it."

"So, it's happy spending, but only if it's not interfering with your savings plan," I offered.

"Exactly."

I wrote it down as 5/5. "Now, what about transit?"

"Ugh. Low. Like, a two."

"You regret transit?"

"Yes. I can always walk or ride my bike. I only take transit when I'm running late or being lazy."

I wrote it down. "And lastly, lunch out at the grocery store."

"Also high? It's the best! Everyone goes for lunch. I only go twice a week. It's a treat."

I showed her the table:

"How many bonus chores did you do last month?" I asked. "Your allowance is $25 a week, $5 to savings and $20 to spending, so $80 is the goal but you spent $150."

	EROI	AMOUNT SPENT/ MONTH
FRAPPUCCINOS	2/5	$30
MOVIES	5/5	$40
CLOTHES AND MAKEUP	5/5	$25
TRANSIT	2/5	$15
LUNCH OUT	5/5	$40
TOTAL		$150

"So many!" she said. "That's why I earned $150. I just also spent it all."

"It looks like if you had to reduce two things, it would be transit and drinks."

"Yes, absolutely."

"What's possible?" I asked.

"Almost all of the cafés. I can grab a tea twice a month. $5 for the whole month is totally possible (savings of $25)."

"What about transit?" I asked.

"Realistically? I think $5 a month is possible (savings of $10)."

"Okay, but if you want to try to save, you have to reduce more. With both unhappy spending categories reduced, your spending would be $115 ($150 – $25 – $10). But you need to live within $80 a month ($20/week) if you want to save the $5 raise each week."

"What if I did this?" she said and leaned in. "I learned that I love the movies, and it's so expensive. I also love clothes and accessories. But I hate not saving. It made me really bummed out. So, what if I use my $20 a week for lunch and the movies only, and then I use bonus money for clothes and accessories?"

"So, you don't buy clothes or accessories until you've earned a bonus chore?"

"Yeah!" she said, excited. "I never want to feel so bummed out about my spending again. I don't need to buy clothes every week. I can wait until I get bonus money. I want to know I can buy them."

"So, you'll save the $5 a week as planned and then use bonus money for shopping."

"Yes," she said proudly.

"I love it," I said.

"Me too. It feels exciting, and I know I can still shop and do things I like, but also that I can't do it with my normal allowance. It's not in my budget. But I can't wait for lunch and movies. They are the things we always do, and I love them."

"I get it. I think this is smart. It's a reduction without making you feel so restricted." I folded my hands on the desk. "This is a great solution, Mia, because overly restrictive budgets can often lead to overspending."

"Totally!" she exclaimed. "I think that's what also kept happening. I'd feel like I missed out on so many things on the weekend when I tried not to spend anything that I'd blow all my money on Monday and Tuesday."

I nodded. "I know that you don't have enough for the dress you wanted, but I really think this was such a good lesson for you and will actually help you stay motivated this time."

She let out a big sigh. "I know. I just really wanted that dress and I thought I could do it. I'm still disappointed. All my friends have these new dresses that they've been trying on and . . ." She shrugged. "I just feel like mine is not special."

"It's hard not to compare ourselves. But how many of your friends just learned one of life's hardest financial lessons this early in life?"

She smiled. "None."

"Exactly!"

"I feel like we should meet again," she said. "In two months or something. To see if I could actually do it and reduce the unhappy spending and save the $5 a week."

"I'd love that. Why don't you talk to your mom about it, and we can go from there."

"I will." She headed out of my office. "Thanks again. I promise I'll save this time."

"Don't promise me. Promise yourself."

She nodded. "I will."

In the waiting room, I met Sofia's eyes and gave her a thumbs-up. I couldn't wait to see how Mia's new plan to reduce unhappy spending and use bonus money for shopping would help her stick to her budget and reach savings goals.

Do You Know Your Stuff?

Test your knowledge with these True or False questions.

QUESTION 1: When you need to reduce spending, it's best to reduce expenses that are 5/5 happy spending.

False. Reduce unhappy spending.

QUESTION 2: Unhappy spending is money spent on something or an experience that we regret later. *True.*

QUESTION 3: Happy spending is money spent on something that has a high emotional return on investment (EROI). *True.*

QUESTION 4: Something with a low emotional return on investment would be a 4/5.

False. A low EROI is 1 or 2.

QUESTION 5: Learning to stop comparing yourself to other people is one of the most important financial lessons. *True.*

HOMEWORK

1. Fill out the budget sheet on the next page.

2. Rate your expenses from 1 to 5 for emotional return on investment.

3. Try to reduce the ones that are ⅕ and ⅖ to come up with money you could save instead of spend!

   QUESTION 1: Which expenses were low EROI?

   _____

   _____

   _____

   QUESTION 2: How much could you reduce your spending with the 1/5 and 2/5 expenses?

   _____

   _____

   _____

MONTHLY EXPENSES	AMOUNT	EROI (1–5)
FIXED EXPENSES		
Rent		
Utility bills		
Cellphone		
Internet		
Insurance payments		
Payments to debt (e.g., student loans, car loans)		
Subscriptions (e.g., streaming, apps)		
Gym membership		
Total Fixed Expenses		
SAVINGS		
Total Long-Term Savings		
Total Short-Term Savings		
SPENDING MONEY		
Groceries		
Gas		
Shopping (e.g., clothing, gifts)		
Transportation (e.g., taxi, transit)		
Entertainment (e.g., books, movies, concerts)		
Meals out		
Total Spending Money		
TOTAL COST OF LIVING		
Surplus/Shortfall		

12

Oliver, Who Made Some Not-So-Good Choices

AGE:	16
SIBLING STATUS:	Only child
INCOME SOURCE:	Not allowed to have a job because he needs to keep his grades up; doesn't need an allowance because he can "get money from my parents whenever I ask"
REGULAR INCOME:	Should be $100 a month (fingers crossed)
CURRENT SAVINGS:	$500 in an online chequing account; an RESP for university (if he gets in); a stock simulator account with $5,000 in it—Oliver makes stock trades to practise, then his dad executes the trades for real in an online investment account that Oliver will have access to when he's 18

I heard a knock and opened the office door with a smile. "Hi, Oliver! How are you?"

He was beaming. "Great."

"Amazing!" I said as we sat down. Then I leaned in. "Did you have the hard conversation with your dad?"

He tilted his head to the side. "No. But I didn't have to. I solved the problem."

"Oh?" I sat back. "Tell me everything!"

He grinned. "I figured out how to make money."

"What?" I asked, confused. "I mean, that's great, but how? Last time you were here, you didn't have access to the accounts and your dad was worried because of the stolen card situation. How did that all get resolved?" Something wasn't adding up.

"It's sports related."

"What do you mean?"

"Does it matter? Isn't it more important that I have my own way to make money now?"

I didn't like it one bit. "Oliver, what's up?" I said it in my most serious, no-BS tone.

He rolled his eyes at me. "It's no big deal, okay?"

"Okay, then tell me what it is," I said impatiently.

He took a moment, then a breath, and said, "Online sports betting."

I felt my heart sink. "Oliver, that is gambling."

"So?" he protested.

"You're not 19!" I said, my surprise still written all over my face.

"Lots of kids my age are into sports betting," he insisted. "It's normal."

It was my turn to take a big breath in and let it out slowly. "How did this happen? You're not even old enough to have an account."

He shrugged. "One of my friends has an older brother."

I put my head in my hands. I was not sure how to go forward or even what to do.

He defended himself. "You know I needed to make income for myself. That I'm not allowed to work."

"Oliver, there are thousands of other ways to make money. This could be dangerous behaviour."

"It's not dangerous. I know what I'm doing."

I shook my head. "How did this even start?"

He paused for a moment. "I had no money. I had to keep borrowing money from my friends, and I wound up owing them, like, $100."

"You borrowed $100 from a friend?" I was surprised because most of the high school students I met with didn't have enough money to lend $100 to a pal.

"Not at first. It was $20 here, $10 there. Eventually, it added up.

What was I supposed to do, not pay them back? I don't want to be that guy."

"So, gambling was the only option?" I asked with a bit of parental tone. I made a note to keep myself in check.

"No. It was sort of an accident the first time. A joke. Like a bet."

"A bet *is* gambling."

He rolled his eyes at me. "We were hanging out, and my friends were all razzing me for borrowing and not paying them back."

"Your friends?" I said, my inability to stay chill about this showing.

"No, it's fine," he insisted. "I had promised to pay them back and I didn't. They think I have access to all this money."

"They don't know the whole picture."

He shook his head. "No. They just see my family, the cars, the vacations and stuff, like when I randomly get handed 50 or 100 bucks. So they think I'm rich and being cheap or something."

"Why don't you tell them the truth?"

His body slumped. Exhausted. "I don't want them to judge my dad or my family. My dad is so weird about money, but I don't want them to judge him. And I don't want to sound like the poor little rich kid stereotype."

I didn't say anything, but I nodded. That part I got. I understood why he didn't want to let everyone into his business. "Okay, then what happened?"

"Well, I only had $20 on me, which was already borrowed. My buddy's older brother said he'd place a bet for me on his account for a UFC fight and then send me the cash if I won. It started as a joke."

"Again. That's a bet. That's gambling."

He ignored me. "But technically, I'm not actually the one gambling."

"I still don't like it. It's real money. You're spending real money on real bets. That's *real gambling*."

"Yeah, but I won huge. I turned the $20 into $80!" He snapped his fingers. "Like that."

"You know gambling is exactly that, right? Gambling? This isn't a way to make money. You are not psychic. That was luck. And luck runs out."

"Well, mine hasn't run out," he said with a smile on his face that made me very nervous.

I covered my eyes with my hands, shook my head, then opened my fingers so one eye was peeking out. "What do you mean?"

"My friend's brother said he'd place bets for me any time. So I took the $80 and made some really great bets. Or, he did—for me. I paid everyone back that day!"

He was thrilled. I was terrified. "You do know that gambling can be highly addictive, right?"

"I'm just using it strategically to pay back my friends—"

"Which you've done," I interrupted.

"And I want to save up $1,000."

My head shot up. "$1,000! Oliver, that's a lot of money!"

"I just don't think that anything will change with my dad. In fact, I think I'll be in more trouble once we have the talk. I'll do it, but I want to ensure I've cashed out first so that I at least have access to money for the rest of the year, and I don't have to borrow anymore."

"I'm worried," I admitted. "What if you start placing bigger and bigger bets to get to $1,000? Gambling can spiral quickly like that."

"I know what I'm doing. I'm making good bets. Not crazy odds. UFC fighters that I know a lot about. Hockey. Things I know."

I gave him "the look." (I use it on my own kids too when I'm not impressed.)

"I'm not the one betting. It's like my dad trading stocks on my behalf. Or like smoking. All of those things are legal once you're old enough, but kids get adults to get stuff for them all the time before they are old enough. If I bought cigarettes, you wouldn't be this worried."

"I would be for your health," I said, meaning it.

He brushed me off. "You know what I mean. And you weren't worried about my dad trading stocks on my behalf. He bought crypto and it crashed! Isn't that the same?"

I truly didn't know what to say. "Oliver, I—"

"Let's just forget that I said anything." He got up and picked up his backpack.

"You don't have to go," I said, looking him right in the eyes.

"I don't want to get in trouble for doing something lots of other kids my age are doing too. Their parents even let them. I'm not even the one doing it, so technically, I'm not doing anything."

I thought for a moment. "Look. We can finish our session today, but please, promise me you'll quit getting this older brother to place bets for you by our next session."

"No," he said defiantly. "This is the first time I've had access to money that doesn't stress me out."

"Oliver, this should stress you out! This is not a way to make money. I have been a financial planner for 20 years—since before you were born—and I'm telling you, this is not a good path. Gambling loops start. Eventually you will lose money. Then you'll try to win it back with bigger and bigger bets."

"I won't do that. I'll quit while I'm ahead."

"You are ahead," I said firmly. "You are. Right now."

He tossed his backpack back on the ground and flopped back into the chair.

"Ugh, this is so annoying," he groaned.

"Well, yeah. It's annoying to be told that your get-rich-quick scheme is gambling."

That made him laugh. Good.

"How much worse do you think that will be if you've been gambling for months and months?"

He rolled his eyes. "Obviously, not good."

"Exactly. Why would you make it worse? Please, listen to me."

He didn't say anything at first. Then, reluctantly he said, "I won't do this forever."

"Please stop by our next session."

"Not the next one," he negotiated. "The last one."

"Oliver. Work with me here!"

"I need time. I can commit to stopping by the last session but not next month."

"Are you going to be a lawyer one day?"

He smiled. "My dad is a lawyer."

We laughed. Hard.

"Okay, let's move on. What questions do you have around budgeting and spending money?" I asked.

"I need to know how a person figures out what they can afford to spend when they have no income, and then all of a sudden lots, but then none again."

I raised my eyebrow at him. "Like if your income comes in big chunks? Randomly? Big ups and downs?"

"Hypothetically."

"Oliver, be real with me. I can't give you good information if you don't tell me your actual question."

"Well, at one point in the last three weeks, I was up a few hundred."

"Okay."

"But I spent it. All. Fast."

"What did you spend it on?" I asked.

"I just went nuts!"

"What do you mean?"

"After I paid all my pals back, I went on a spending spree. I spent money on things I never spend money on, or would never."

"Like what?"

He thought for a moment. "Like, I bought all my friends lunch. I bought a new basketball. I bought video games. Ice cream. Coffee. It didn't matter. I spent it all. No limit!" He was saying it like he wasn't happy about it, but his expression was wide-eyed with awe.

I nodded. "You splurged."

He let out a big breath. "I splurged. I didn't know how to stop it."

"Do you know why this happened?" I asked.

He shook his head. "No willpower?"

"There's a reason you had no willpower."

"What's that?"

"You've been living without access to any spending money for a while. Think of it as living in scarcity. A situation where everything is out of reach financially. With adults, it's usually a feeling of being broke for a long time. Of not having enough money to enjoy anything for a long time, then eventually, you just kind of give up and spend. With adults, that usually happens on credit cards."

"Like, I don't have enough money, so what's the point in trying to budget?"

"Exactly," I said. "You have had a taste of that at a young age. Then, when you got money, you blew it all at once."

"That makes sense. I don't have access to the spending money, so I always feel broke, and borrowing from pals made me so tired of having no money. So when I got it, I just went wild."

I nodded.

"So how do I plan a budget for next time, so I don't do that?" he asked.

"The problem is, you don't really know what you'll make, do you?" He shook his head.

"So, the only way to deal with that is to add up what you plan to spend, set the realistic intention to limit yourself to that amount, and then hold any extra aside when you get paid."

"What do you mean, plan to spend?"

"Well, for you, we don't want to plan a budget around what you just spent. Your splurge. We want to plan a budget around what you realistically need per month."

"Oh, I get it. And I'm sure it should be somewhere between splurge and scarcity."

I smiled. "That's the sweet spot."

He nodded.

"Let's start with some of the expenses you'd like to be able to spend money on. On average, in a month."

He thought about it. "I think the $100 a month that we used before would actually be enough." He got a bit sheepish. "Maybe $150. Actually. One thing I learned when I had access to money is that because I haven't had it for so long, I forgot about normal things that I would actually like to spend money on."

"Why don't you tell me how you'd spend it?"

"Probably $50 for shopping. Same for food and movies and stuff."

We wrote it out.

"You don't have a Hard Limit," I said.

"What's that?"

"The lesson I was going to teach you today," I said with a smile. "It's the line between the money you can and cannot spend when you get paid. Usually, the money you cannot spend is bills and savings."

"But I don't have any bills or the ability to save right now because we don't know what I'm going to make?"

Oliver's Simplified Budget Worksheet

MONTHLY INCOME	$0
MONTHLY EXPENSES	
FIXED EXPENSES	$0
Rent	$0
Utility bills	$0
Cellphone	$0
Internet	$0
Insurance payments	$0
Payments to debt (e.g., student loans, car loans)	$0
Subscriptions (e.g., streaming, apps)	$0
Gym membership	$0
Total Fixed Expenses	$0
SAVINGS	
Total Long-Term Savings	$0
Total Short-Term Savings	$0
SPENDING MONEY	
Groceries	$0
Gas	$0
Shopping (e.g., clothing, gifts)	$50
Transportation (e.g., taxi, transit)	
Entertainment (e.g., books, movies, concerts)	$50
Meals out	$50
Total Spending Money	$150
TOTAL EXPENSES	$150
Surplus/Shortfall	–$150

"That's right."

I showed him this.

MONEY YOU CANNOT SPEND: $0	MONEY YOU CAN SPEND: $150 HARD LIMIT
Fixed Expenses: $0	Spending Money: $150
Long-Term Savings: $0	
Short-Term Savings: $0	

"The first $150 you make would be put aside for spending. Then, you'd save everything else."

"Got it. So, if I cash in $200, I put $150 aside for next month, and save $50?"

"Correct. With these kinds of budgets, you have to guess on the savings, but limit the spending."

He nodded. "$150 would feel really good."

"Can I ask how much you spent last month? To compare?"

He looked embarrassed. "$225."

"An expensive lesson in scarcity mindset. One that is important to learn so you recognize when the urge to splurge is coming as a rebellion to the scarcity you've felt."

"I'm going to have the hard conversation with my dad," he said out of nowhere.

"Where did that come from?" I asked.

"I need to be allowed to get a real job. I want to make my own money."

"I know you do. Look how far out of your way you are going just to avoid having that difficult conversation with him."

He shrugged. "Yep."

I didn't say anything.

He sighed. "I know. I know. I don't know why I can't do it. I've started it so many times, and then I chicken out when he starts freaking out."

"Maybe you could write him a letter," I said. "Sometimes, that's a good way of saying what we want to say and ensuring that our words are heard and also not twisted. Especially if someone is likely to have a strong reaction."

"Dear Dad. You're impossible to talk to about money. I'm gambling. Give me money. Love, Oliver," he said dryly.

I raised an eyebrow. "Don't forget stealing," I joked.

He laughed. "Oh, he never will."

"Oliver, if you stop betting now, at this moment, then at least it's not something you continued to do."

He shrugged.

"I don't know your dad, but I can't imagine he'd think he was helping you if he knew the lengths you were going to in order to get money, or the relationship with money that you're developing here."

"Yeah, I know. Things aren't great with my dad right now. He already thinks I'm sneaking around, being a bad kid. I don't want things to get worse."

I smiled. "That counts. You don't want things to get worse, so the worst-case scenario is that it stays the same."

He didn't say anything.

"Write him the letter."

He nodded and stood up. "I'll try."

"And I'm happy you'll stop the betting and tell your parents. Gambling is not investing. It's not a way to make money, and the long-term addiction can be detrimental to your future in so many ways."

He nodded again. "I know. It was fun having money. But you're right. It's not sustainable. Or I don't want it to be sustainable."

"Good luck," I said.

"You say that every time," he said.

"Because what you're about to do is hard."

He left my office, and my stomach was in knots. I hoped he knew what he was doing.

Do You Know Your Stuff?

Test your knowledge with these True or False questions.

QUESTION 1: Your Hard Limit is the difference between the money you can and cannot spend each pay period. *True.*

QUESTION 2: Scarcity mindset is good for finances.

False. Often, scarcity mindset can lead to overspending.

QUESTION 3: Writing a letter can be a great way to say what you want to say about your finances to kick-start an important money conversation. *True.*

QUESTION 4: Gambling is investing.

FALSE! False, false, false. Trying to earn money quickly often means taking big risks that are akin to gambling. Please don't gamble your hard-earned money.

QUESTION 5: Luck runs out. *True.*

HOMEWORK

Earning more money is a great way to help you reach your goals. Brainstorm five side hustles that you could do and how much money you think you could make from them.

For example, you could mow the lawn for $10 per mow, 10 times a year. This gives you $100 ($10 x 10).

PART 4
Enjoy Your Money

What Money Skill Do You Need to Learn Next?

How to enjoy your money! Sounds easy, right? You may be thinking, "Oh, I already know how to do that. Not enjoying my money is the goal." If this is true then I'm sorry to tell you, that's the start of a bad relationship with money. The goal is not to stop enjoying your money. But that doesn't mean spending without limits.

When I say enjoy your money, what I mean is "maintain a positive relationship with money," one that will work for you now, when you're older, and for the rest of your life. Over the years, your financial situation will change more times than you can imagine. Sometimes it will feel great, easy. Sometimes it will feel awful and hard. That's normal. Money is never a "set and forget" situation.

Maintaining a positive relationship with your money is an essential skill so you don't end up resenting your financial life, feeling stressed out, and at worst, sinking into debt.

Why Is Enjoying Your Money an Important Skill?

Did you know that in a 2024 survey done by FP Canada,[†] 44% of Canadians lose sleep over their money? That's almost half the country! Our financial health definitely impacts our mental health.

I think many financial books miss this part of the education. But learning to enjoy your money is a hugely important part of doing well with your finances for life. Over the years, I've seen that people who have a good relationship with money can roll with the ups and downs better. They are more confident in their decisions, and they have hope for the future.

Those who have negative relationships with money are constantly stressed (whether they need to be or not), live with deep regrets, and resent their financial situation. They don't feel secure and they don't feel happy about their finances, which leads to feeling broke all the time. When people feel broke all the time, they eventually overspend because they believe there is no point in trying. They give up!

How Will You Use This Skill in the Future?

Having a good relationship with money is the key to sustaining long-term financial plans. It's the key to rolling with the ups and downs life will throw at you, and it's the key to making confident financial decisions now and in the future.

It's a skill you'll use every day: In how you talk to yourself about money (self-worth). In how you communicate with others about money (honest without judgment). And in the role money plays in your life (does it define you or is it a tool?).

---

† FP Canada Financial Stress Index

What You Will Learn Throughout Part 4

- How to start and maintain a good relationship with money

- How to have realistic financial expectations

- How to give yourself permission to enjoy your money

- How to stop comparing yourself to others and appreciate what you have

- How to have hard money conversations

I think this may be the most important part of the entire book.

Safe and Happy: Both, at the Same Time

The key to having a good relationship with money is to always strive to feel both safe and happy with your finances, safe being the obvious of the two. Here are some of the safety measures we often think of when we think of finances:

- Don't overspend; avoid consumer debt (credit cards) whenever possible.

- Save for short-term spikes (so, have money saved for emergencies).

- Live within your means (ideally, this means keeping your fixed costs low).

- Save for the long term—this improves your financial future!

We just spent the first three parts of this book talking about these pillars of financial wellness. So why aren't these enough?

Lots of people I work with have all the "right" things in place with their finances. They don't have consumer debt, they saved up money for emergencies, and they live within their means so that they can save for retirement one day. Why are these people still unhappy with their financial situations? Why do they have bad relationships with their money? Because being safe is not enough. You have to be safe and happy—both at the same time.

Most people aren't rich. Maybe you think they are, but they probably aren't. Only 7.6% of adult Canadians have a net worth over a million dollars.[†] Keep in mind too, that number includes their house. So, if their net worth is $1,500,000, they are considered a millionaire in that survey. But if their house is worth $1,000,000 of that, then really, they have $500,000 in savings and a house.

That's a lot of money, but it's not a millionaire in the way we think of it. They don't have a million dollars in a bank account. If housing weren't included, I'm sure there would be far fewer millionaires in Canada.

Life is expensive. Most people in this country, 96%, are not "rich." If someone doesn't have credit card debt, it means they are living within their means. They aren't overspending. Do you know what that also means? They say no a lot. No to trips that they wish they could take. No to clothes that they wish they could buy. No to concerts they would have loved to go to. They say no to things they can't afford. It's hard, and it can feel gross if you feel like you say no too much.

Feeling safe with your finances means that you live within your means. Feeling happy with your finances means that you live within your means without hating your life. That's safe and happy at the same time, and it's the building block for growing your money.

So far, we've talked about how the first thing to do is earn money, because without an income, the rest of the book doesn't matter. Once you establish your income, you learn how to save. Then how to budget, the living within your means part. But you need to make sure that you can do that and do it happily. If not, your best savings and budgeting habits will likely fall off the

---

† FP Canada Financial Stress Index

rails, because if you constantly feel broke, eventually you might just give up trying.

Striving to feel both safe and happy at the same time is the key to having a good relationship with money.

You do this in the following ways:

- Be realistic about what you can and can't afford.

- Make sure you spend money on things that bring you joy.

- Don't compare yourself to other people.

- Know how to have hard conversations about money.

13

David, Who Missed

AGE:	15 (just had a birthday)
SIBLING STATUS:	Has a younger brother
INCOME SOURCE(S):	Old enough to legally work but hasn't found a job; random jobs in the neighbourhood
REGULAR INCOME CALCULATION:	$200 in the next 4 weeks
CURRENT SAVINGS:	$0 in sock drawer
SAVING:	$0

The last time we spoke, David left feeling confident about a new plan he had in mind to ask his mom for a small extension to repay her by the end of summer. I was looking forward to seeing how it all worked out but was surprised to see David back on my porch only three weeks later.

We sat down and I jumped right in. "How's the debt plan going?"

The smile faded. "Not good."

"Oh no! What happened?"

"I asked her for the extra time to pay it off. She agreed and we reduced my payment to her from $60 a week to $40 a week as long as everything was paid off by the end of August."

I was nodding along.

"So, everything was good at first. She wasn't going to charge me interest. But I couldn't keep up the $40 a week. I missed each (2) payment! I still owe $240."

He was so bummed out. Eyes cast down. Big frown. Usually David was so upbeat. I hadn't seen him like this.

"What's your mom's take?" I asked.

"She's mad. She knows I need another extension and wants me to make the plan with you." Then his shoulders hunched down even more. "She took the console away until I'm paid back."

"Ouch," I said.

"Yeah, I'm embarrassed," he admitted.

My heart broke for him. "This is a really tough financial life lesson you're learning."

"I know, but I wish it wasn't a life lesson with my mom involved. I lost her trust."

I didn't say anything.

"And the console," he said, lightening the mood.

"There's a way to gain it back," I said. "Both the trust and the console."

He finally looked up.

"We need a plan you can actually stick to. Better to pay it slowly and actually do it than promise the world and not deliver."

He nodded solemnly.

I leaned toward him. "David, you're a hard-working kid who is very motivated. You're young. This will be fine."

He sighed and put his hands on his knees, maybe wiping sweat off them. "I guess."

I sat back and moved the air in front of us around, as if to change the energy in the room. "Let's take a step back. Did anything about the plan work?"

"The first week was okay, but then I couldn't stick to it. Again."

"Why do you think that happened?"

"I just wasn't realistic. About anything."

"What do you mean?"

"That's what got me into this mess, isn't it? Being unrealistic?"

I waited for him to go on.

"I was overly optimistic. About everything."

"What specifically?"

He looked down at the floor. "I wasn't realistic about how little I could actually spend in order to pay back my mom the first or the second time. Especially the first time. I wasn't realistic about how much I could earn either. And . . ." He paused and I could see how difficult this was to say. "It was completely unrealistic to think I could afford the console so early. I was way too optimistic. Like, unrealistic."

"That's a lot to carry on your shoulders," I said.

"Well, it's my fault. I wouldn't wait for the console, so then I had to ask my mom to wait. I couldn't wait but she has to. It's not fair to her, and now I don't even have the console."

"This is what debt allows us to do. Have things right away that we shouldn't because we can't really afford it. It's a problem that grown-ups also have all the time. Not being able to wait. No delayed gratification. We all struggle with it from time to time."

"I've learned my lesson," he said. "I'll just have to be rich one day and not worry about it." He said it sort of joking, but it had an angry tone.

"What do you think rich is?" I asked, curiously.

"Having lots of money."

"What is 'lots of money'?" I asked.

He sort of smiled at the question. "Um. Like, I don't know, being a billionaire?"

My stomach squeezed. A billionaire. "A billion dollars is a lot of money."

He shrugged. "Yeah, but there are so many billionaires in the world."

"There are just over three thousand. Worldwide. That's roughly 0.0000375% of the population."

"Wow. That's actually not that many."

I shook my head. "No. A billion dollars is an amount of money we toss around like it's a million, but it's very different."

He nodded, but I could tell he wasn't truly convinced.

"Okay, let's say you wanted to earn a billion dollars over your lifetime."

He smiled. "I do."

"Then let's map out the difference in earning a million versus earning a billion in your working life."

He perked up.

"Let's say the average person works for 40 years," I continued. "From 25 to 65 years old."

He nodded.

"To earn one million over the 40 years, you'd have to have an average income of $25,000 a year."

"That's it?"

He seemed stunned.

"Yep. But that's also the amount you'd have to save in order to have one million dollars available after you retire."

"So if I wanted to *save* and not just earn a million dollars, I'd have to earn way more so I could save $25,000 a year for 40 years."

"Technically you could probably save a bit less and grow your money with investments (more on that in Part 5), but if you saved $25,000 a year for 40 years, you'd save one million."

"That actually feels really exciting. That I can earn one million dollars over my working life."

"Earning it is one thing. Saving it is another."

He grinned. "And not spending it all."

"That's the game."

"What about a billion?"

"Get this," I said. "If you wanted to earn one billion dollars over the same 40 years, you'd have to earn $25 million a year for 40 years."

His mouth shot open. "For real?"

"For real. $25 million. Per. Year."

He sat there. A bit stunned. "Whoa."

"*Whoa* is right. The jump from $100 million to a billion is also huge. If you wanted to earn $100 million over your 40 years, you'd have to earn $2.5 million a year."

"That's more what I was expecting. Like, earning a ton of money, but not $25 million a year for 40 years."

"A billion dollars is one thousand million. One thousand million!"

"Okay, okay," he said, laughing. "I get it."

"I'm not trying to deter you from setting high goals for yourself. You're a smart kid. Maybe a billion is in your future, but part of having a good relationship with money is being realistic about stuff. Not negative, just realistic."

"Right. Negative would be like, 'I'll never earn anything.' Unrealistic is like what I did when I thought I'd earn more this summer."

"Exactly. Setting realistic goals for ourselves helps us feel good about our finances because we aren't setting ourselves up for failure. If we set unrealistic goals for our incomes or savings, and then if we can't reach them, we feel like a failure, even though you maybe did a great job."

"Maybe my goal in life is to earn enough money so that I can save $25,000 a year?"

He said it like a question.

"Well, you could set that as a goal, but I don't love setting life financial goals with numbers."

"Why not?"

"Because numbers mean something different to everyone. One person may need $100,000 to feel rich. Another person may need one million. It all depends."

"True. True."

"So, let me ask you, what would rich allow you to do?"

"If I was rich, I wouldn't have to worry about money."

"Then *that's* the goal."

"Yeah. I know money is a thing people worry about. It stresses them out. They have to work jobs they hate. They can't buy homes. I want to be rich so I don't have to worry about that stuff."

I had been writing it all down. "Maybe I can rephrase." I turned the screen toward him. "David's financial life goal is to earn enough income so that he can buy a home, have enough money to pay for bills and fun, and save. Plus, enough emergency savings so that he has job flexibility." I looked at him. "How's that?"

He smiled. "That's accurate."

"It's not about being rich, David. It's about feeling safe and happy with your finances."

"Safe meaning 'having enough'?" he asked.

"Yeah. Safe, because you earn enough to live your life and put money aside for both short- and long-term savings."

"And happy meaning 'enjoying money'?" he asked. "Like, going on trips, buying cars?"

"Exactly," I said. "We are not just here to save every penny. It's about the balance. Earning enough to pay your bills and save, but also spending money on things that give you joy."

"And safe and happy is different for everyone," he said.

I nodded. "One hundred percent."

We sat there for a moment. Letting it all sink in.

"So, I'm not safe or happy with my money right now. Because of the debt to my mom."

"For the moment, that's correct. But that doesn't mean we give up. It means we find our way back to safe and happy." I folded my hands in my lap. "What does 'safe' mean to you?"

"Safe means being debt-free to my mom and to my friend who is still waiting for the $20."

"And what does 'happy' mean?"

"Saving up money again. Getting the console back. Still buying things I love, but waiting until I can actually afford them. Realistically. That would make me happy."

"Delayed gratification is like that. It helps us be safe and happy at the same time. Safe because we don't overspend, and happy because it makes something special. Like we've earned it. There's a sense of pride."

He sat another moment, then looked over at me. "I have to ask my mom if I can lower the weekly payments again, this time to $20 a week instead of $40, and extend the loan out until the end of September."

"That's the realistic amount?" I asked.

He nodded.

"How do you think she will take it?"

"I think it's better than missing more payments and avoiding her."

"That tracks," I said.

"Once both my mom and my friend are paid back, I need to save again."

"You can turn the minimum weekly payments to Mom into minimum weekly savings for you."

He smiled. "Savings for me. I like that."

As David left the porch, I told him I'd be happy to sit down again once he started saving up. I was confident he'd be okay. He had realistic income targets now, realistic spending goals, and realistic expectations around what he could and couldn't afford. What a great lesson in how to have a good relationship with money.

We all mess up sometimes. That's normal. No one is perfect. The important thing is to not lose hope and to keep trying to get back to safe and happy.

Do You Know Your Stuff?

Test your knowledge with these True or False questions.

QUESTION 1: Earning and saving money are the same thing.

False. Earning money doesn't mean you're saving money. But you can't save money unless you earn it.

QUESTION 2: Having debt means you failed at money.

FALSE Sometimes debt happens. It isn't something to be scared of in life, just something that really needs to be planned properly before you take it on. You want to make sure it's for the right reasons.

QUESTION 3: Some debt, like credit cards, charges high interest.
True.

QUESTION 4: No one is perfect. *True.*

QUESTION 5: Hope is important for our finances so we don't give up. *True.*

HOMEWORK

Write one or two sentences answering the following questions.

WHAT DOES LONG-TERM FINANCIAL SUCCESS LOOK LIKE TO YOU?

_____
_____
_____

WHAT IS "ENOUGH MONEY"?

_____
_____
_____

HOW DOES WAITING FOR SOMETHING MAKE IT FEEL SPECIAL?

_____
_____
_____

WHAT DOES IT MEAN TO BE RICH?

_____
_____
_____

14

Tania, Who Finally Flew

AGE:	18
SIBLING STATUS:	Has a younger brother
INCOME SOURCE:	Job at the local arena
REGULAR INCOME CALCULATION:	$2,248 in the next 4 weeks
CURRENT SAVINGS:	$0
SAVINGS GOAL:	Post-secondary school

I got an email from Tania the week she was on her trip. It was a photo of her with her grandmother on a balcony. Palm trees in the background. She looked so happy! They both did.

In her email, she asked if we could meet one last time so she could get her final question for me answered: how to grow her money. We booked the meeting for about a month after she got home from her trip.

When the camera came on, I couldn't believe my eyes. Tania looked the same, but something was very different. She was smiling. A huge grin on her face. She was sitting up straight and confidently.

"Wow!" I said. "You seem really good."

She kept smiling and shrugged. "The trip changed me."

I was thrilled for her. "I could not be happier."

"Me neither. It honestly changed my life. I can't believe I almost didn't go!"

"You were very nervous about using your savings and taking on debt."

"I know. But the happiness from this trip was so high. I could never have an experience like that ever again. Worth it. Totally worth it!"

She was so enthusiastic it was contagious!

"I'm so happy for you," I said again.

"The plan worked. So realistic. So doable. It feels like magic. Like, I got to go and I still get to live."

"That's the beauty of a realistic plan. It makes you feel safe and happy. Both at the same time."

"What do you mean?"

"Financially safe. You're not putting yourself in a situation where you overspend on a credit card and can't pay it back within three months. And you're not reducing your spending so much that it isn't realistic. Plus, you're still paying back the savings for school."

"Right. So it was financially savvy."

"Definitely. And it was also happy."

She beamed. "So happy."

I smiled back. "I think one of the things you asked about in our first meeting was how to never spend money."

She blushed. "I know."

"How does that sit now, from this perspective?"

"Spending money is fun," she said, almost like it was a confession.

"It is! But only when you know you're okay financially too. Plus, you spent it on something with a very high emotional rate of return. I don't know if you'd feel this free and happy about your finances if you spent it on something you regretted or if you overspent and now still had credit card debt."

She was quick to jump in. "No, definitely not. But I did get a taste for permission."

"That's an interesting term. Permission. What do you mean?"

She took a big breath. "Like, permission to not be scared of spending money. That's what you gave me."

My heart swelled. "I didn't give you that. You earned it yourself."

"You know what I mean. I expected us to sit down and hammer out a plan where I'd be miserable for years so I don't pay a dollar in interest, but really, the fear was so over the top. Not necessary."

"Worst-case scenario living."

"Exactly. And things for me are actually not bad. I'm saving so much money."

"This is one of the key parts to having a good relationship with money," I said. "Enjoying it. Most people have the opposite problem as you. They spend too much. They need to work on the safe part. You needed to work on the enjoyment part. The happy part."

"I don't want to ever live the way I was, being so scared of money. Thinking I'm bad with money all the time."

"Oh my God, Tania, you're too good with money. I'm just glad you recognize this now. The negative self-talk."

"What do you mean?"

"One of the main things I listen for when people are meeting with me is how they talk about money when they relate it to themselves now and their future. Things like 'I suck at money,' or 'Money just doesn't make sense to me,' or 'I will never make money' show me that their financial confidence is low and that they are starting to develop a bad relationship with money."

"Why does that matter? Like, the relationship with money?"

"We make money decisions every single day. Money is how we achieve our hopes, dreams, and goals. If you think that money is something to be terrified of, like it's this awful thing never to be enjoyed, every day is going to be stressful. If you think you're bad at money, then ultimately, you're saying you're bad at life. If you're always stressed about money, you're always stressed about life."

"Not good for mental health."

"Exactly. Financial stress bleeds into all areas of our life and robs us of joy and peace."

"That's so true. I feel less stressed than ever, even though I have less spending money than before and I ate into my savings. Weird, eh?"

"Why do you think that is?"

She thought about this for a moment. "I think because it wasn't as scary as I thought it was."

"Can you expand on that a little?"

"I took money out of savings and used a credit card for the trip. It was on purpose, for a good purpose, and I feel really in control. I have no regrets with it."

"So, how does this help you on your money journey going forward?" I asked.

She gave a small smile. "You're not gonna like this."

"Why's that?"

"I want to go back. To Bermuda. Every year. My soul is happier knowing that it's possible."

"Something to save for," I said.

"Exactly. But how do I do that?" She searched for the word. "Safely?"

"I think it means less savings for school each year. Which will mean a bit of student debt."

She took a sharp breath in. "How much? Like, how much is safe?"

"Let's have a look!" I opened up her savings sheet. "How much each year to go to Bermuda?"

"I think $3,000. I could stay with my grandmother, and I don't have to rent a car next time. A lot of the extra money was because of the car rental and the grad trip."

I nodded. "If you remember, you were just about breaking even after the trip. We reduced your spending by $40 a month to pay back the $2,501 you used for the trip over 62 months."

I reshared the screen from our last meeting.

Tania's Long-Term Savings, Updated after Trip

	LONG-TERM SAVINGS	SCHOOL EXPENSES	SPENDING MONEY	LONG-TERM SAVINGS BALANCE
PHASE 1: PART-TIME BEFORE SCHOOL	~~To save Jan–June (Phase 1) $89 x 24 weeks~~			~~$2,136~~
PHASE 2: JULY	$1,870 – $365 = $1,505			$1,505
PHASE 2: FULL-TIME BEFORE SCHOOL	$1,870/month for 13 months			$24,310
YEAR 1	+$10,256 (from income)	–$12,500	–$4,536	$19,035
YEAR 2	+$10,256 (from income)	–$12,500	–$4,536	$12,255
YEAR 3	+$10,256 (from income	–$12,500	–$4,536	$5,475
YEAR 4	+$10,256 (from income)	–$12,500	–$4,536	–$1,305

"This still gave you some spending money, but it was still tight with $4,536 per year instead of the original $5,016, which was $378 per month. To make room for an additional $3,000 of short-term savings per year, you'd have to reduce spending money by $250 per month ($3,000/12 months), but you already only have $245," I said.

"What if I got raises? I usually get an inflation raise every year."

"I'd use that to increase spending money, because your spending money is likely to go up by inflation too."

She nodded. "That makes sense. So what do I do?"

"The only way to do this is to keep saving like you're saving now and then use $3,000 a year from your savings. That means your spending money goes up from $4,536 ($378 per month) per year to $7,536 because you're spending an extra $3,000 a year."

Tania's Long-Term Savings, Updated for Future Trips

	LONG-TERM SAVINGS	SCHOOL EXPENSES	SPENDING MONEY	LONG-TERM SAVINGS BALANCE
PHASE 2: JULY	$1,870 – $365 = $1,505			$1,505
PHASE 2: FULL-TIME BEFORE SCHOOL	$1,870/month for 13 months			$24,310
YEAR 1	+$10,256 (from income)	–$12,500	–$7,536	$16,035
YEAR 2	+$10,256 (from income)	–$12,500	–$7,536	$6,255
YEAR 3	+$10,256 (from income	–$12,500	–$7,536	–$3,525
YEAR 4	+$10,256 (from income)	–$12,500	–$7,536	–$13,305

I showed her the updated chart. "It means you'd graduate with $13,305 of student debt."

She squinted into the screen. "The negative $3,525. That's the amount I'd need to start taking from debt in Year 3."

"Yeah. That will be your first year of shortfall. The negative $3,525 would start in your third year, and then you'd add in $10,256 from work, then spend $12,500 for tuition and books and $7,536 in spending to end up with $13,305 in debt at the end of Year 4."

She thought for a moment. "Basically, the entire $13,305 is Bermuda."

I sighed. "Pretty much. The $3,000 times four years is $12,000 of the shortfall."

She sat back and folded her arms. "I'd qualify for government student loans."*

"You probably would, given your family income. I can't guarantee, but it's likely."

"I already did some of the estimates, and it looks like I'd qualify for $15,000. I didn't want to use debt at first, but now I'm not so sure."

This was interesting. What a change from her outlook only a few months ago.

"Do you feel safe and happy taking on student debt for travel?" I asked carefully.

"That's where you come in. You told me, when I used the credit card, that anything on a credit card I could pay off within three months was acceptable."

"That's my rule. Yep."

"So, what is the rule for government student debt?"

"I can't answer that. Some people will have student debt for years, but that doesn't mean it was a bad decision to go to school. Student debt is not the same as consumer debt. It's part of that investment in your future cash flow. Also, some student loans are entirely interest-free. It really depends."

"What if I continued to live at home, working full-time after I finish school? And put the original $1,870 I used to save for school onto the debt?" she asked.

I calculated. "To be conservative, I'll assume you don't have a fully interest-free loan. I'll assume that your student loan will be interest-free up to six months after school.* You'd be debt-free in just over seven months after graduation ($1,870 x 7.5 months = $14,025).''

She was thrilled.

"And, if you planned to live at home for one year after graduation and could work full-time, saving the $1,870 a month, you'd pay off the student debt for seven to eight months and then save the $1,870 for the other four to five months and have a nest egg of at least $7,480."

"Then, I get to move out. If affordable housing ever becomes a real thing."

I held my crossed fingers up. "I think this definitely gives you a good start."

"So, it's okay to enjoy some of this money I've been working so hard to save." It was a statement, not a question.

I nodded. "Because you've got a plan that's safe and a really high emotional return on investment."

"Travel made me feel like a different person."

"I think you are a different person now."

She smiled. "So, tell me how to grow this money."

I laughed. Stay tuned to see how I answer this question in the final part of Tania's story.

CHAPTER 14 NITTY GRITTY

Qualifying for Government Student Loans

- Government student loans are student loans provided by the government for you to attend post-secondary education.

- Some portions of these loans may be entirely interest-free. It depends on where you live in Canada, what the current government policy is, and what portion of your loan is federal versus provincial.

- They provide many programs to help you repay the loan, such as Repayment Assistance and Payment-Free Loans while you're in school and six months after.

- You have to qualify to get one.

- For more information about eligibility, read here: https://www .csnpe-nslsc.canada.ca/en/home.

Do You Know Your Stuff?

Test your knowledge with these True or False questions.

QUESTION 1: Negative self-talk can impact our relationship with money. *True.*

QUESTION 2: Our relationship with money doesn't matter.

False. If you have a good relationship with money, it means you feel confident that you can make good financial decisions, and that makes you feel confident in life.

QUESTION 3: If you buy something on a credit card but can't pay it off right away, you can't buy it.

False. A good rule of thumb is that a big purchase that goes on your credit card needs a plan to be totally paid off within three months.

QUESTION 4: This book is so helpful! *True.* ☺

QUESTION 5: It's okay to enjoy your money. *True.*

HOMEWORK

Any time you catch yourself speaking negatively to yourself about your ability to do math, work with numbers, remember money lessons, or budget, remember that negative money self-talk can often become self-fulfilling prophecy. Try reframing:

INSTEAD OF SAYING:	TRY:
"I'm bad with money."	"I find budgeting really difficult. It takes more willpower than I'd like, but I can do it."
"I'm never going to make enough money to enjoy my life."	"Life is expensive. But I am young, and I have my whole life ahead of me. Lots can change between now and adulthood. I'm not going to give up."

15

Mia, Who Learned a Big Lesson

AGE:	13
SIBLING STATUS:	Middle kid between two sisters
INCOME SOURCE:	Has a regular allowance
CURRENT SAVINGS:	$40

I met with Mia two months after her grade 8 grad. Sofia, Mia's mom, was there, but didn't come in this time. She gave me a big thumbs-up when Mia walked into my office.

"Hey, Mia!" I said excitedly as she sat down. She looked happy. Very different from the last time.

"Hi!" she said warmly.

"How was graduation?" I asked. "Can you believe you start high school in a couple weeks?"

She broke into a smile. "I know! It's wild. Grad was also great." She paused. "Even without the dress."

I smiled. "I'm glad. What did you end up wearing?"

She pulled out her phone. "A dress that my sister Bianca wore to one of her semi-formal dances."

I looked at the photo. She looked beautiful and, more importantly, truly happy. She scrolled through some more photos of her and her pals in their formal wear. I couldn't help but smile.

"You look like you're having a wonderful time," I said.

"We did. It was so fun. Kinda sad too. I cried." She laughed out loud. "All my friends did."

"You cried?"

"Yeah. It's over. The end of an era. Some of my friends will go to a different high school than me. I've been at the same school with some of them since kindergarten."

I nodded. "That is the end of an era."

She gave a fake cry and put her hand on her heart. "I know. Honestly, I know the other dress was special, but I do love this one. I got so many compliments on my sister's dress. No one even knew that it wasn't a new one."

"Why would it matter if they did?"

"I don't know." She paused. "I think I thought having a new dress would make graduation feel more special?" She said it as a question.

"But it doesn't look like it was any less special wearing one your sister already wore."

"No! It was amazing. It was new to me and also free. Win-win."

"That's very different than your perspective a few months ago."

She giggled. "I know. I was really obsessed with that blue dress."

"What has helped you feel good about your choice to wear your sister's dress and not feel resentful of it?"

"Because now I know it actually didn't matter."

"What do you mean?"

"Part of the fun leading up to grad was looking at all these dresses online with my friends and sort of picturing what we were going to wear. We would pick out dresses online and stuff. Talk about how our hair was going to be. Make a style board."

I nodded.

"I got caught up in that part. It was fun! So much of the buildup was based on what we would wear. I would have felt boring if I'd just said I was wearing my sister's dress."

Oof. "Feeling boring is one of the main reasons people overspend these days."

"Oh yeah?"

"In my experience, yes. I believe it's because social media is such a big part of our lives. People want to post interesting things. Things they are doing, things they are wearing. But of course, things cost money."

"They sure do." She tilted her head to the side. "I think you're right actually. About social media."

"What makes you say that?"

"Well, after our last meeting, I was so bummed that I couldn't get the dress that I turned off my social media and the grad group chat for the week leading up to graduation."

"You turned them off?"

She smiled. "I muted."

"That's hard to do."

"It was actually. But it was my mom who pointed out how I'd been feeling really great about wearing Bianca's dress, dancing around the house, taking photos, planning my hair. But I wouldn't send photos to my friends in the group chat, and when I read about their stuff on my phone or went on social media and saw photos, I'd feel mad about it."

"Mad?"

"Yeah. I'd start feeling like I needed the new one, and I'd start begging my mom to buy me a new dress."

"So your mom saw that when you'd go on your phone, your mood changed from excited to angry about your financial situation."

"Like, instantly!" she exclaimed.

"That's the same with many adults," I said.

"It is?"

"Oh, yes. Me included. Social media can really make us feel low about our finances, even when things are good."

"I guess so. I mean, I've heard that before, but I always pictured people who were trolling influencers and being upset that they didn't have a yacht."

"No, no. I mean, I'm sure that exists, but I'm talking about everyday people. Saying no to overspending is hard, and social media makes it feel harder."

"What do you mean?"

"If you're saying no to overspending," I said, "what are the things you're usually saying no to?"

She thought for a moment. "Um, clothes. Lunches out, takeout. Movies, makeup. I don't know, fun!"

"Exactly! We can't opt out of our bills. We always have to pay rent, phone bills, et cetera. You will too one day. So, whatever is left of our money after we pay our bills is our spending money. We only have so much, right? Which means we have to say no to things in order to live within our means and not go into debt."

"So why does social media make us spend more money? The ads?"

"The targeted ads don't help things. But truly, it's social media that makes saying no to overspending much harder." She looked skeptical so I tried another route. "Imagine this. Your friends are all going to a concert."

"Okay. So, this must have been before the cost of a concert was the same as someone's monthly rent."

I laughed. "I know, right? Let's say you're invited, but you really can't afford to go, because concerts have become so expensive. If you go, you won't have enough money to pay your bills."

"Hypothetically, right? I mean, I don't have bills yet."

"Hypothetically," I agreed. "So, let's imagine you say no to your friends. And you feel proud about that. You set a solid financial boundary to keep your finances safe. You feel good."

"That's good."

"That's great."

"Is it Taylor Swift?"

I laughed again. "Sure. But then, you're scrolling through your phone and every single one of your pals, and even people that aren't your pals, are posting about how excited they are to go to this exact concert you chose to say no to."

"FOMO," she observed.

"Big time," I agreed. "So now, the FOMO you feel is heightened every time you are on your phone. Painfully aware of all that you're missing out on. How do you think you feel about your financial boundary at that moment?"

"Angry."

"You bet. Even resentful. Thoughts like 'Why am I so broke?' and 'How can they afford to do this?' and of course 'This isn't fair' race around inside your brain. A bunch of harmful self-talk creeps in when you start feeling resentful about your financial situation."

"That literally happened to me with the dress. I was having these catty thoughts about my friends too. Like, 'I hope their dress doesn't look as good on,'" she said in a fake snobby voice. Then she held up one hand as if to say STOP and put the other on her heart. "Like, excuse me? Who do I think I am?"

"FOMO leads to resentment, which leads to jealousy. It can make us feel and say things that aren't really who we are."

She screwed up her nose. "Gross."

"It can be. Social media has a way of taking a healthy financial boundary, like I shouldn't spend on that, and turning it into a resentful moment. Or encouraging us to give in to the pressure and overspend."

"Because if someone doesn't want to feel jealous or resentful, or FOMO, they just spend."

"They just spend."

She gave a nervous chuckle. "So, you either feel left out and keep your finances in check, or you spend too much and feel gross about that later."

"You just hit the nail on the head. Social media can really impact our relationship with money and make us feel like we can't afford to have fun."

"But we can. I had a great time in a free dress."

"There are definitely ways of enjoying life that don't necessarily beg for a social media highlight reel."

She smiled. "But I love some parts of social media. Some of it is so funny. It's also how we hang out a lot."

"That's okay. I'm not saying social media will ruin your finances. I'm saying it can lead to resentment of your finances and suck the fun out of the money you do have if it leads to constant comparison. Being aware of that is the most important thing."

"Like, how my mom pointed out how angry I was after reading the chat or being on social."

"Exactly."

"So, I don't have to quit social media in order to have a successful financial life," she joked.

"No, you don't! But I think being aware of the impact it has on your financial happiness is important. To have a good relationship with money, you need to make financial decisions that leave you feeling both safe and happy. Not one or the other."

"And social media makes the happy part harder."

"That's right."

"Maybe I should just take a break from socials when I start feeling anxious about my finances or when I've said no to something I can't afford."

"That's a great idea. Many of my adult clients go on social media detoxes for two or three weeks when they are trying to set financial boundaries and want to feel good about them and not resentful. They like feeling safe and happy."

She nodded. "I like that."

"Which part?" I asked.

"The safe and happy motto."

"It's a good one."

"But what happens if you actually can't afford anything?" she asked. "Like, if you are actually broke? How do you grow your money so you can afford to have a bit of fun and pay for your life?"

"We'll talk about that next time." I walked her to the door, wished her and Sofia goodbye, and couldn't help smiling as they walked away.

Do You Know Your Stuff?

Test your knowledge with these True or False questions.

QUESTION 1: A good relationship with money is important for financial success. *True.*

QUESTION 2: Feeling boring or inadequate can lead to overspending. *True.*

QUESTION 3: Social media does not make it easy to spend money. *False.* Targeted ads and a sense of missing out make you want to spend money you may not have.

QUESTION 4: Feeling broke is hard. *True!*

QUESTION 5: Temporarily muting or unfollowing people who make you feel resentful about your finances can be helpful for your relationship with money. *True.*

HOMEWORK

Take a social media detox.

1. Next time you're feeling frustrated that you can't afford to pay for something, make sure you aren't scrolling through social media feeds of people who are able to afford the exact thing you're trying to avoid spending money on.

2. Mute people who make you feel inadequate, jealous, or boring. Those feelings can lead to overspending and resentment over your finances.

16

Oliver, Who Got in Big Trouble

AGE:	16
SIBLING STATUS:	Only child
INCOME SOURCE:	Not allowed to have a job because he needs to keep his grades up; doesn't need an allowance because he can "get money from my parents whenever I ask"
REGULAR INCOME:	Should be $100 a month (fingers crossed)
CURRENT SAVINGS:	$500 in an online chequing account; an RESP for university (if he gets in); a stock simulator account with $5,000 in it—Oliver makes stock trades to practise, then his dad executes the trades for real in an online investment account that Oliver will have access to when he's 18

One minute before Oliver's session, I received an email from him. In the subject line were just two words: "Dad's coming."

I heard them arguing in the hallway. I took a big breath and opened the door.

"I'm so sorry," Oliver said as he pushed past me into the office.

"Are you the financial planner?" Oliver's dad asked me, out of breath.

I nodded. "Yes. Are you John?"

"I am." He was still catching his breath.

"I'm Shannon." I put out my hand. He took it, and we shook. He had a solid handshake. The kind that reminded me of meeting bankers on Bay Street at the start of my career. "It's nice to meet you. Please come in and sit down. Can I get you a glass of water?"

"Yes, that would be great. Oliver too."

"I'm fine, Dad," he said in an irritated tone.

"It's a pitcher," I offered. "So we can all help ourselves."

I left to fill up my water jug and my stomach was in knots. I didn't know what to expect. When I came back in, they were both sitting down. Not speaking. Oliver was glaring at the floor. I filled everyone's glasses and sat down.

"Well. This was unexpected," I said, hoping to lighten the mood.

No one laughed.

"For real, though," I said. "This was unexpected. John, I'm happy to meet you. As you know, I've been conducting research for a financial book, and after interviewing Oliver, he asked to set up financial coaching sessions." I looked at Oliver. "Oliver, because you are my client, I have to make sure you are okay if we chat here with your dad in the room?"

"Yes," he said in a disgruntled tone. "It's fine."

"Listen," John said, "I'm not here to ruin your research or your coaching. I'm here to add to them. To set the story straight." He took a big sip of water. "You must think I'm an awful parent the way this one"—he motioned toward his son—"has probably gone on about me."

"I don't at all," I assured him.

Oliver rolled his eyes and shook his head. His jaw was tight. He didn't look at me.

"Just before I was supposed to drop him off here, his mother and I found $300 in Oliver's drawer."

"You were spying," Oliver spat out.

"Mom was putting laundry away," John corrected.

Oliver shrugged. "Whatever."

John looked at me. "I'm not sure if Oliver told you, but not too long ago, he actually stole my debit card and took money out—$100."

Oliver looked at me.

"Go on," I said.

"Of course, since then, we've been monitoring him closely. I didn't raise him to steal and lie. Especially about money."

He seemed genuinely distressed. Like he had no idea how this happened or why. I felt for both of them.

"When we found $300 in his drawer," he continued, "we obviously knew he'd been stealing again or doing something dishonest."

"I told you I didn't steal it," Oliver snarled. "I made it! I don't steal!"

"You most certainly stole money from me!" John snapped back.

"It's my money!" Oliver roared. Then he looked at me. "Do you see what I'm dealing with?"

Uh-oh.

"Tell me, Oliver," John said. "What exactly are you dealing with? Parents who have given you absolutely everything? Who try to teach you how to be a good person? To start your life off on the right foot? To not have to worry about anything so you can focus on school and get into a good university? Yes. Tell us, Oliver, what hardships are you dealing with?"

Oliver's eyes filled with tears. He didn't say anything. I think he was afraid that if he spoke he'd cry.

"Obviously, things are really tense right now," I continued. "I think you both need to calm down, go home, and talk this out."

"I'd like to discuss this here. The whole way over here, he's acting like he's some sort of victim here. Like he's so hard done by. Did he tell you that I'm the bad guy here?" He shot a look to Oliver. "*You* steal and *I'm* the villain."

"John, please," I said. "You know that I have been talking to Oliver for months. The picture that I have is not of an ungrateful child who wants to steal money. To make bad choices for sport? Not even close."

Oliver continued to stare silently at the wall. John sat back in his chair. He also didn't say anything.

I continued, "What I know about your son is that there is a reasonable explanation for all of this. The $100 from the chequing account and where I think the $300 cash came from. A reason that I believe he has been avoiding talking to you about."

John looked insulted. He turned to Oliver. "How can that be?"

Oliver looked at me. "Can you tell him?"

"Tell me what!" John demanded.

I shook my head. "Oliver, if you want to be understood here, you're going to have to have that hard money conversation." I turned to his dad. "I've been a financial planner for a long time. I know you want what's best for your son. I can see that. On the other hand, the way you want to help Oliver doesn't seem to be working. I think we can all agree on that?"

I looked at them both. No one responded, which I took as a cue to keep going.

"In my regular job, this is quite common. A sort of misalignment of money personalities or financial habits between people. One person thinks things should be done this way, the other disagrees. When this happens within families, it can create really bad financial dynamics in the household. Which leads to a terrible relationship with money for both."

"You probably think this because he didn't tell you the truth. How much help we give him. How much money we have put aside."

"Dad, I told her everything."

"And I'm glad you did. I'm sure she knows plenty of teenagers who would wish that they could be in your shoes with parents who strive for the best for them."

"That's only partially true," I said. John's eyes widened, but he said nothing and I continued. "Over the past several months, one of the reoccurring themes in the coaching sessions I've had with Oliver is that he feels stressed out about how to gain access to the money you have so generously put aside for him."

"But—" John interrupted, but I cut him off.

"Please let me finish." He cleared his throat and stayed silent. "One of the main efforts he's been focusing on is how to have a hard money conversation with you."

"With me?" John asked, surprised.

"Yes. With you."

He looked at Oliver. "You know I'm always happy to teach you about money."

"Teaching me is not talking to me," Oliver said.

"Oliver, John," I said before John could interject, "you're welcome to have that conversation here, or we can end the session for today."

John spoke first. "I'd like to continue. I'd like to hear what Oliver has to say and obviously I'm not capable of doing this at home."

"Everyone is capable of having healthy and also hard conversations about money with people they love. But there are a few steps I can offer up to aid things along. Does that sound good?"

Oliver actually cracked a smile, and I felt like John might actually be open to listening.

"Step 1," I continued. "When having a hard money conversation, make sure everyone has eaten and isn't dehydrated."

"Are you joking?" Oliver asked.

"Not at all! If you're hungry or your blood sugar is low, you're not in a great headspace to have a tough conversation."

They both nodded, as if to say, "That makes sense." Because it did.

"Assuming we are all good there?" I asked.

They nodded.

"Okay, Step 2 is using respectful language. There will be no yelling, blaming, or shaming. When having a tough money conversation, the last thing anyone needs is to feel blamed or shamed. It's tough or hard because you both already feel like you're right. That's why it's a hard conversation. This isn't about being right—it's about finding middle ground. No one will win."

John sat back. I could see he wasn't convinced, but he was listening.

"Step 3. Everyone gets a turn to voice their side without being interrupted. Make sense?"

They both nodded.

"Okay!" I said enthusiastically. "Oliver, do you want to go first?"

"Sure," he said quietly. He didn't say anything for a long while. Then he looked at me and shrugged.

"Maybe I'll lead with a question," I offered. I didn't waste time getting to it. "Oliver, why don't you tell your dad why you felt like you had to take the debit card and pull the $100 out without asking."

I saw him wince. It was very direct, but hey, when it comes to hard money conversations, being respectful and direct is exactly the right balance.

"I needed the money," he said so quietly, it was almost inaudible.

"What did you need the money for?" I asked.

I saw John's back straighten right up. Oliver took a deep breath in and sighed loudly.

"Lunch," he said, matter-of-factly.

"That's ridiculous!" John exploded. "You're lying."

"See?" Oliver said and looked at me.

"John, please. No interrupting, remember?"

"But it's absurd. He has access to money for lunch. All he has to do is ask!"

"I do ask," Oliver spat back. "But you don't give me the money for it."

"When? When was the last time you asked for lunch money that I withheld from you?"

Oliver scoffed at this. "The last time I dared ask! A few months ago. You gave me the debit card to go to the movies with Omar. Remember?" I could see John thinking. "I held on to the card so I could use it for lunch that week. I bought two lunches on it. Remember? One sub. One hamburger. Remember?"

"I do," John answered, irritated. "You didn't return the card after the movie when you were supposed to. And you did this so that you could spend too much money on overpriced garbage food. Yes. I recall, Oliver."

"Isn't that money supposed to be for Oliver to spend on lunch?"

"The money is for Oliver to spend on things he needs," John said. "When he needs them. Just because we have the money doesn't mean he should be wasting it on expensive takeout. He can pack a beautiful and free lunch at home every day. One of the first things I did when I wanted to get serious about my money was to stop eating takeout food and coffee. I saved up enough money for a down payment. Not $15 on a designer hamburger, I can tell you that much. This generation doesn't know how to save and go without. I'm trying to teach Oliver that."

"In your opinion, what are some items that Oliver can spend the money on?"

He cleared his throat. "Lots of things. Like I said, whatever he needs."

"Could you give me some examples?" I asked carefully.

"Any time he needs to replace his sporting equipment." He was looking to Oliver to agree. Oliver said nothing, so we all took that as an agreement.

"What else?" I asked.

"Excursions with his friends. They went to one of those arcade places. He had the card. I even drove them there last year before any of them had a licence."

"What about clothing?" I asked.

"Yes, of course. If he needs something, we provide it. In fact, we provided that in addition to this spending money. He wouldn't even need to use the card."

"But he'd still need to ask, right?"

"Well, his mother and I can't know all the things that he wishes he could wear."

"That's true," I said. "Oliver, do you want to chime in here?"

"Dad. You say the money in the account is spending money, but you rarely let me spend it. When I do, you monitor it and get mad at me for it. Even something like buying lunch—because you don't like it. If it's supposed to be my spending money, I should be able to spend it however I want to. Obviously on legal things."

"But you keep lying and sneaking around, so we are monitoring or keeping the card for your own safety."

"I'm lying and sneaking around because, no matter what I buy, you're going to get mad at me and withhold the card!" He was getting louder. "I took the card and the $100 because I didn't want to hear you go on and on about how you saved your lunch money and bought a house. Dad, this isn't the 80s. I can't buy a house because I don't go out for lunch."

"I think this discussion is really important," I interrupted. "For both of you."

I turned to Oliver. "Oliver, it sounds like you believe that the lying and sneaking around is a result of the monitoring and withholding of money."

"Yes. It's the only reason."

"And John. You believe that you are monitoring and withholding as a result of the lying and sneaking around."

"Yes."

"Do you both see the chicken and egg scenario here?"

They both smiled a bit.

"No wonder things are getting tense," I said. "You're both right, and you're both wrong."

"Oliver," John said, "I'm not trying to be withholding. I'm trying to teach you and help you."

"Yeah, but you don't even let me have a chance to learn. How can I practise saving or spending properly if I don't have money to save or spend?"

"We worry. That's all."

"I know," Oliver said, his tone warming. "But I hate having to ask you for the card. I hate it. It feels like jail. Like you don't trust me."

"I—I," John stuttered a bit. "I do trust you."

"I don't think you actually do," Oliver said.

John let out a breath. "I want to trust you. But now there's been the stealing of the card and this $300 that you still haven't explained. It's hard to trust when these things are happening."

"Those are both because I hate asking you for the card and you won't let me work to earn my own money. If you let me earn my own money with a job, I wouldn't even have to ask."

"But you need good grades to get into university. You're already struggling to find time for homework between extracurriculars and tutoring."

"Then you need to give me access to the account and an allowance," Oliver said in a no-nonsense tone.

"But what if you just waste it away?" John said.

"But what if I don't?" Oliver said. "What if I actually learn how to spend and save and live within a budget. Because I'm practising."

I could see this resonate with John.

"Where did you get the $300?"

Oliver looked at me, and I gave him a small nod.

"I had a friend's brother put money down on some UFC fights. I won a bunch."

"Gambling!" John said, outraged. "Oliver, who are you?"

Oliver put his hands up. "I know, I know, I've learned my lesson."

"How so?" I butted in.

"I used to have $800."

"What!" John and I said in unison.

Oliver let out a big sigh. "I was trying to get to $1,000 so that I could have some spending money for the rest of the year without having to ask you for the card."

John was beside himself. "I cannot believe that you'd gamble. Where did you even get the money? Was that part of the $100?"

"No, no," Oliver said. "I borrowed money from friends."

"Oh, that's just lovely. Borrowing from your friends to gamble."

"Listen, some of them do it with their own dads."

"Are you still doing this?" John demanded.

"No." He looked down at the floor. "I made three terrible bets and kept upping the ante, trying to win it back. Now I only have $300. I lost big time."

"Oliver," I said, "that's an important lesson."

"Yeah. I got it."

John gave his head a shake. "Look. I understand that maybe I've been overly protective and made it hard for you to ask for money when you need it. For that, I apologize. But I can't believe that you'd go to these lengths just to avoid speaking to me about it."

"I tried, Dad. But you'd always freak out right away. I tried. I really did." Oliver's voice wavered. "I'm not a bad kid. I promise."

John swallowed hard and put his hand on Oliver's back.

I let the silence hang for a moment before speaking.

"So, this is Step 4, where you each say what you need and why you need it. John, why don't you start."

He shut his eyes and finally opened them when he spoke. "I need to be able to stop worrying that Oliver will spend all the money and be irresponsible."

"Why do you need that?"

"Because he's my son and I love him, and I know how hard it is to make it out there financially. The game for this generation is different than mine. I do know that. He's got to learn how to go without and to make smart choices and not be spoiled."

"What I'm hearing," I said, "is that you need to be able to give him the control of the money without the anxiety that it will never be enough."

"Yes," John said, almost relieved. "That's exactly it."

"Oliver, what do you need?" I asked.

"I need to be in control of my own spending money so I can practise and learn these things without feeling guilty or dumb every time I make a decision."

"You need to be able to have control of the money without worrying about being shamed," I said.

"Yes," Oliver said.

"Good stuff. Now we move to Step 5. A solution." I turned to John. "What do you think would help you give control of the card to Oliver without worry?"

He thought about this. "Maybe if there was a limit to what he could spend. So even if it went to zero, it would be a good check-in?"

I nodded. "And what happens after a few months when the $500 goes to zero? How does it get replenished?"

"Maybe an allowance is what he needs," John said.

"I would love an allowance," Oliver said. "Please. I want to work. I want to make money."

"How about this," I said. "John, if you were willing to give an allowance, say $150 a month"—I made eye contact with Oliver, then turned back to his dad—"you could fill the account up monthly, and then you wouldn't have to worry because the total damage, or worst-case scenario, would be that Oliver runs out of money halfway through the month. But there's a limit to the losses."

John nodded.

"Oliver, what do you think is a good solution?"

"I'd love a monthly allowance. $150 would be incredible, and as long as I don't run out, I don't want to be monitored anymore."

"But what if you run out?" John asked.

"Fine. If I run out halfway through the month, we can sit down and go over it. But otherwise, leave it alone. Let me spend the money how I need to spend the money. As long as I'm not overspending the $150 per month, who cares?"

I could see John mulling it over.

"So, the card would go to Oliver," I said. "An automatic $150 would transfer from John to Oliver on the first of every month. No monitoring whatsoever *unless* the $150 isn't enough."

They both nodded.

"What about large-ticket purchases?" Oliver asked. "Like a new coat. That kind of thing?"

"Your mother and I will still help with those purchases," John said.

"So, the money in that account is strictly spending money," I confirmed. "Lunches, entertainment, day-to-day stuff."

"Yes." John paused. "And I'd like to see some savings habits too."

"Tell me about what you'd like to see," I said.

"If this is all about the opportunity to practise living with a budget, shouldn't he also be practising saving?"

I raised my eyebrow and looked at Oliver. He smiled.

"It will be. I'll save up part of the $150 for big purchases, or things I'll need money for down the line."

"How much?" John asked.

"How about $30 a month?" Oliver suggested.

John thought it over. "So, you save $30 a month of the $150, and I leave you be, unless you run out of money."

Oliver broke into a wide smile. "That would be amazing. Honestly, it would change my life."

"Oliver," I said, "does this solution make you feel both financially safe and also emotionally happy?"

"Definitely." He could barely contain his excitement.

"John," I said, "does this solution make you feel both financially safe and also emotionally happy?"

"Yes," he said and took a big breath. His shoulders relaxed. He turned to Oliver. "I wish we had done this much sooner. Before the lying and the sneaking around."

"Me too," Oliver said. "I'm sorry."

"I'm sorry too," John said.

I smiled. "Well, congrats, you two. You just had a very successful hard conversation about money."

They both sort of rolled their eyes, but with smiles.

"These are important skills," I said. "We downplay the importance of having a good relationship with money. We think it's secondary sometimes, to the budgeting and savings habits, but it's not. Someone with great habits can still fall way off the rails or be unhappy with their financial lot because of how they feel about their situation."

"Thank you," John said to me. "This makes it very clear."

"I'm so glad." I smiled.

"It would make a good story for your book," John said, and we all laughed.

I was thrilled for Oliver and for John! What a wonderful breakthrough for them both. It was my last session with Oliver, and I have to say, I was hoping that one day he'd come back to tell me how it all played out.

"This is our last session, Oliver. I know we've tackled a lot of topics. Is there anything else that you have questions about? Regarding your finances?"

He looked at his dad. Then to me.

"Is crypto a good investment?"

My eyes widened and a mischievous grin spread across his face. Find out why in the final Oliver chapter!

Do You Know Your Stuff?

Test your knowledge with these True or False questions.

QUESTION 1: Money conversations can be tough to have. *True!*

QUESTION 2: Everyone should be hungry and thirsty before an important money talk.

False. Literally the worst! Make sure everyone can be their best self.

QUESTION 3: Someone is right and someone is wrong.

False. The reason it's a fight is because each person involved thinks they are right, or at least has a reason for why they are behaving a certain way. Find out why. What's underneath the action?

QUESTION 4: Everyone should feel excited about the solution! *True.*

QUESTION 5: A solution is something that makes both people feel financially safe and emotionally happy, even if they had to compromise. *True.*

HOMEWORK

If there's something to do with money that you really want to talk to someone about, now's your chance. Use the steps outlined in this chapter to do it!

WHAT PERSON A NEEDS	WHAT PERSON B NEEDS

Step 4:

_____

_____

_____

Step 5:

What can Person A compromise on to help Person B with their needs?

_____

_____

_____

What can person B compromise on to help Person A with their needs?

_____

_____

_____

Solution:

_____

_____

_____

PART 5
Grow Your Money

What Money Skill Do You Need to Learn Next?

The last financial skill you need to learn is how to grow your money. What do I mean by that? Let's say you've saved $20, and without adding any additional money to your savings, the $20 turns into $22. Like magic.

You just made $2!

Growing your money is not really magic; it's passive income that you make from investing. Investing can mean a whole bunch of things. It can mean putting money into stocks and bonds, a business, or a bank account that pays you interest. Basically, you take your money, put it somewhere, and hope that you'll get more money without doing anything but taking a risk.

Why Is Growing Your Money an Important Skill?

There's only so much money we can earn and save. That's why we need to try to make our money work for us too. If you're able to grow your money over time, you won't have to save as much, which means you won't have to earn as much, which means you won't have to work as much. Growing your money allows you to reach your financial goals more easily.

How Will You Use This Skill in the Future?

Whether you're saving for a down payment, a big trip, or retirement one day, the more you can make your money grow, the faster you'll reach your goals!

What You Will Learn Throughout Part 5

- The difference between saving money and investing money

- Compound interest versus investing versus gambling

- Risk tolerance and time horizon

- Social media and its impact on investing

17

David, Who Was Well on His Way

AGE:	15
SIBLING STATUS:	Has a younger brother
INCOME SOURCE(S):	Old enough to legally work but hasn't found a job; random jobs in the neighbourhood
REGULAR INCOME CALCULATION:	$200 in the next 4 weeks
CURRENT SAVINGS:	$0

Just after school started, I met with David to check in on everything. Since our last meeting, he had paid his mom the $20 a week they had agreed upon. But because he stretched out the payments a second time, she ended up charging him interest and penalties!

"Your mom charged you interest, did she?" I asked.

"Yep." His eyebrows went up. "She still has the console, and she charged me $5 per missed payment plus interest."

"Yikes," I said. "What interest rate did she charge you?"

"20%," he said. "Same as a credit card."

I scrunched my face and shoulders up. "That's tough, but fair."

"Well, now I'm worried it's going to take me even longer to pay back."

"That's what interest does. When it's debt, it makes your life harder.

When it's savings, it actually helps you. Interest is your best friend or your worst enemy."

"Yes, I actually ended up paying more than $500 for the console. Because of the interest and penalties."

"Exactly. You still had $240 to repay Mom last time you were here. She added $10 in penalties for the two missed payments and 20% interest on the outstanding balance of $250 ($240 + $10)?"

He nodded. "Yep. She said she wanted the interest to be charged like a credit card."

"Credit card interest isn't charged monthly, it's daily on the amounts you haven't paid off by the due date. So, if the rate is 20%, you take 20% and divide by 365 days in the year, and then multiply by the average daily balance you carried that month (0.20/365)."

"Oh. I think she did it weekly."

"Okay," I said. "So, 20% divided by 52 weeks in a year would be 0.384% per week."

"I think so?" He pulled out his phone. "Here's what she made me as a schedule. I think she rounded a bit."

I looked it over. "This is a great chart. You can clearly see that you paid $6.69 extra in interest, so it took you an extra week to pay off that plus the $10 in penalties."

"I'm glad it was only $6.69. But can you imagine if I owed, like, $2,000?"

I quickly calculated. "I estimate that you'd pay over $500 in interest and take about 44 weeks to pay it off."

"Yeah, it's crazy how the interest makes everything cost more. Seems unfair."

"On the other hand, once you're debt-free, you can make interest work for you."

"Like, investing?"

"Sort of," I said. "Compound interest is your friend. It helps your

WEEKS	DEBT	INTEREST FOR ONE WEEK (0.384%)	TOTAL AMOUNT OWING	TOTAL PAYMENT	BALANCING OWING
1	$250	$0.96	$250.96	$20	$230.96
2	$230.96	$0.89	$231.84	$20	$211.84
3	$211.84	$0.81	$212.66	$20	$192.66
4	$192.66	$0.74	$193.40	$20	$173.40
5	$173.40	$0.67	$174.06	$20	$154.06
6	$154.06	$0.59	$154.65	$20	$134.65
7	$134.65	$0.52	$135.17	$20	$115.17
8	$115.17	$0.44	$115.61	$20	$95.61
9	$95.61	$0.37	$95.98	$20	$75.98
10	$75.98	$0.29	$76.27	$20	$56.27
11	$56.27	$0.22	$56.48	$20	$36.48
12	$36.48	$0.14	$36.62	$20	$16.62
13	$16.62	$0.06	$16.69	$20	-$3.31
TOTAL		$6.69			

savings grow for no reason in the same way interest on debt grows for no reason."

He smiled. "Using it as a force of good versus evil."

"Exactly, young grasshopper." I opened my laptop and made a new chart for him. "Imagine that the $250 you had was actually savings and that you were saving $20 a week instead of paying down debt. Plus, imagine an annual interest rate of 3% paid out monthly, but the interest was working for you in a high-interest account for four months."

I showed him the math.

MONTHS	SAVINGS	INTEREST (0.25%/MONTH)	TOTAL SAVED	NEW SAVINGS	BALANCE SAVED
1	$250	$0.63	$250.63	$20	$270.63
2	$270.63	$0.68	$271.30	$20	$291.30
3	$291.30	$0.73	$292.03	$20	$312.03
4	$312.03	$0.78	$312.81	$20	$332.81

"Over approximately the same period, you'd save $80 by putting $20 a week aside for four months. If you added $80 plus the original $250, you'd have $330. But, because of compound interest, you have $332.81—$2.81 more than you saved!"

He didn't look impressed. "Is $2.81 all I would earn?"

"Remember that you only paid $6.69 in interest to your mom. The more money you save or spend, the more interest has an impact. Plus, the longer you have debt or the longer you save, the bigger the compounding."

He looked at it and nodded. "I see it. It's compounded because I earn interest on interest."

I beamed. "Exactly. Compound interest is when you earn interest on the money you've saved and on the interest you earn along the way."

"Because in month one, I earned $0.63 and also added $20 but in month two, I earned interest on the full $270.63, which includes that $0.63 of interest from the month before. So I technically earned interest on the interest. Like, free money on free money."

"You got it," I said. "That's why people don't keep their money under their mattress."

He nodded. "That's cool."

I felt like I had unlocked a mystery of the world for him.

"Is this investing?" he asked.

"Sort of. This is an example of a high-interest savings account. You can also get interest like this in something called a GIC."

He nodded. "My grandma has those, but I don't know what they are."

"A GIC is called a Guaranteed Investment Certificate. You put your money into an account with a financial institution like a bank or credit union. They take that money, hold it for a period of time, and guarantee you get the initial money you deposited back plus whatever interest. So there's no risk. It's guaranteed."

He scrunched up his face. "But you're saying that's not really an investment. Even though it says investment in the name?"

Hmmm. That was a great question. "To me," I said, "this is still a form of guaranteed income. Like a high-interest savings account. If you put $1,000 into a GIC, it will never be $999. It will never lose money, but you also won't get that much free money from interest."

"Not the 20% my mom charged."

I laughed. "Definitely not. The job of high-interest savings accounts and GICs is to keep pace with inflation. So, if inflation is around 2%, then a high-interest savings account should offer around 2%. Right now, inflation is high, so interest rates for GICs and high-interest savings accounts are higher than normal. Not 20%, though. But the goal isn't to beat inflation."

"Low risk. Low reward," he said.

"Sort of, yeah."

"But still helpful."

"Oh yes! This is a great way to start your money growing for you. You earn money without having to save more or work more. Plus, it's guaranteed!"

"Am I too young to have a savings account or a GIC?"

"You are. Right now, in Canada, you have to be 18 to have a high-interest savings account or GIC. But financial companies are always innovating, so this may not be forever. You should always check and see if there are youth accounts available for savings as well as chequing."

He looked bummed. "So, how can I grow my money until I'm 18?"

"The only way is to get a grown-up you trust, like a parent or family member, to put it into an interest-paying account on your behalf. The other thing you can do is figure out how to create passive income on your own."

"Passive, like, I don't have to work to make it?"

"Yeah. Passive income is income generated by something other than employment. Investing is a really common way of doing this. The amazing thing about investing, or compound interest, is the idea that you put money somewhere and hopefully it comes back to you as more money, but you didn't have to work more or save more."

"What would make passive income for an adult besides investing in stocks and bonds?"

I thought for a moment. "Passive income can also be from real estate. A lot of adults will earn passive income by investing in real estate. Maybe they purchase a house and rent it out. If the house costs them $2,000 a month for mortgage, taxes, et cetera, and the rent is $3,000 a month, they make $1,000 a month. Does that make sense?"

He thought about it. "Yes. The work they did was to make enough money to buy the house. Then once they bought it, or invested in it, they earn the $1,000 per month without doing more than just sort of maintaining it for the people who live there."

"Right. Also, some people will invest in a business. They take money, invest it in a person or a business, and hope to earn more back without actually being materially involved in the business."

"Like a big tech start-up or something?"

"Yeah! Or even smaller businesses. Maybe even their own business."

"What do you mean?"

I could see this had piqued his entrepreneurial spirit. "Where do you get your hair cut?" I asked.

He was confused by my question but answered, "There's a barber I go to on Bloor Street."

"Does the barber you go to own the barbershop?"

"No, his dad owns it. He works there."

"What's his name?"

"Nick."

"So, Nick cuts your hair. You, or your parents, pay $40 for the cut at the checkout."

He nodded.

"Did the $40 go to Nick? Or did it go to the barbershop as a business?"

He thought for a moment. "The business."

"Right. So how much do you think Nick made from cutting your hair?"

He smiled. "I don't know, but less than $40."

"I agree. Maybe he made $15 for the haircut."

David nodded. "Makes sense. So after his dad paid Nick $15, the remaining $25 ($40 – $15) was passive income to his dad?"

"Not exactly. Probably $20 from every haircut goes back into the business to pay for rent, supplies, bills. That kind of overhead."

I could see him working it out. "So, the passive money is $5 a haircut ($40 – $15 – $20)."

"Exactly."

"And he's got at least three other people working there in a day."

"How many haircuts are each of them doing a day?" I asked.

"Maybe six?"

"So what's his passive income? Or profit?"

He thought out loud as he punched numbers into his calculator.

"Okay, $5 times three people times six haircuts is $90 a day ($5 x 6 cuts x 3 people)."

"Times six days a week?"

"So, $90 times six is $540 a week. And times 52 weeks in a year is . . . $28,080 a year."

"Right! So, investing the $15 in Nick is a good investment for the owner because Nick is happy with his $15, the business overhead is covered, and Nick's dad makes some passive profit because he didn't have to cut the hair himself."

I could see the wheels turning. "What if I did this with my dog-walking?" David asked. "Like, get another person in another neighbourhood?"

"Go on," I said.

"Like, what if I charged $10 to take a dog out for a big walk and go to the dog park, invested in someone by paying them $6, and made $4 for every walk."

"Does that feel like you're making your money work for you?" I asked with a smile.

"Yes!" he said. "I already know someone who would be happy to do that for $6 and who lives in a neighbourhood where there are lots of dogs. He just doesn't want to put the time in to find the customers."

"That's where your upfront time investment will come in," I said. "There's nothing really passive about passive income in business, but often the investment is your time, and hopefully, much of it is upfront."

He punched something into his calculator. "If I had him do two walks a week, that's $8 a week for me, which is $32 a month ($8 x 4 weeks)!"

"That certainly seems like a good way to grow your money." I was so proud of him.

He looked proud too.

"I'll be done with my loan to my mom around the holidays. Maybe I'll make this my New Year's resolution. I'll take all the passive income from dog-walking and save it."

"I love that."

"Me too."

"Do you think it's realistic?" I asked with a smile. "All things considered?"

"I don't think two new customers a week is realistic right at the start. But maybe after a few months."

I nodded.

He sighed. "The bigger lesson for me is not to spend the money before I've earned it. Then it's okay if it takes a little bit longer to get to where I want to be."

"You've come so far," I said in a wise old woman voice.

David smiled. "I finally feel good about my money."

"That's amazing. What do you think is the biggest lesson for you?"

He sat back. "All of it. Tracking it. Setting realistic earning, savings, and spending goals." He lowered his voice. "How debt becomes real scary real quick."

"When we started this whole journey, you said you wanted to be smart with your money."

He nodded, remembering. "I did say that, didn't I?"

"My big question for you, then, is do you feel like you're being smart with your money now?"

"I do. Definitely. I know now that being smart with my money isn't just about earning it or saving it. It's about knowing what's coming in and what has to go out, and having the patience and willpower to save it."

"So much of money is a waiting game, and not much is instant. But the more time you have, the more you can earn, save, and grow."

"Good thing time is on my side."

This was the last of our sit-down meetings for this book. David is still the side hustle king of the neighbourhood. I still see him babysitting, dog-walking, and shovelling, and I know I'll see him again in the future for a financial session. Probably when he's a successful entrepreneur and wants to start investing in more businesses. He is armed with the skills he needs to be financially successful. He knows how to track his income, set savings goals, live within his means to avoid debt, and grow his money—all while making sure he enjoys it. I can't wait to see where he ends up!

Do You Know Your Stuff?

Test your knowledge with these True or False questions.

QUESTION 1: Credit card interest isn't charged monthly, it's daily.

True.

QUESTION 2: Compound interest is dividends from investing in stocks.

False. Compound interest is when you earn interest on the money you've saved and on the interest you earn along the way.

QUESTION 3: A Guaranteed Investment Certificate (GIC) has risk.

False. A Guaranteed Investment Certificate (GIC) has no risk. You put your money into an account with a financial institution like a bank or trust company. They take that money, hold it for a period of time, and guarantee you get the initial money you deposited back plus whatever interest.

QUESTION 4: The job of high-interest savings accounts and GICs is to keep pace with inflation. *True.*

QUESTION 5: Passive income is a bonus from employment.

False. Passive income is income generated from somewhere other than an employer or a contractor.

HOMEWORK

Calculate how much you'd pay in credit card interest if the rate was 20%, you had a balance of $1,000 for the full 30-day billing cycle, and you didn't pay it off.

Solution:

STEP 1: Calculate your daily rate.

20%/365 days = 0.0547% daily rate

STEP 2: Calculate how much interest in a billing cycle.

30 x 0.054795% x $1,000 = $16.44

Tania, Who Felt Like She Had It All

AGE:	18
SIBLING STATUS:	Has a younger brother
INCOME SOURCE:	Job at the local arena
REGULAR INCOME CALCULATION:	$2,248 in the next 4 weeks
CURRENT SAVINGS:	$0
SAVING FOR:	School and travel

Since our first meeting in January, Tania had graduated high school, started full-time work, and made a savings plan to be in as little debt as possible after school while also travelling to see her grandmother yearly. It was like she had been transformed.

"Travel made me feel like a different person," she said.

"I think you are a different person now," I said.

She smiled. "So, tell me how to grow this money."

I laughed. "I believe that was one of your questions on your initial intake form with me in January."

I heard her clicking around on her screen. Then she smiled. "Good memory!" she said. "It's right there. My last question."

"When you say 'grow this money,' what exactly do you mean?" I asked.

She sat back. "Isn't it when your money makes more money for you?"

"It can be. Or at least, that's what it's supposed to be. You invest money and then take more out later even though you didn't put any more money in."

She thought about that. "Is that why everyone says real estate is an investment? Like a house? Like, you buy a house for $500,000 10 years ago, and today it's worth a million dollars even though you didn't spend more than $500,000."

"Real estate is one example."

"Or even investments? Like people who bought Apple stock in the 80s and now have millions?"

"That's an example of extreme returns. Much of that is luck."

"Well, I could use some luck," she said. "Or at least, no bad luck."

"Tell me what you mean by that."

She tilted her head. "I've heard of people investing money in, like, stocks and losing so much. I don't want that."

"Again, a lot of those stories are also extremes. You're 18 now, and you are old enough to invest. Are you thinking you'd like to invest your money?"

I saw her squirm a bit.

"You look uncomfortable with the idea," I said.

"No, no, I'm just scared."

"What are you scared of?"

"I work so hard for every dollar. I don't think I could handle it going down."

I nodded. "I want you to think about this. Is the pain of losing $1 greater than the potential for you to earn $3?"

She looked confused.

"Let me try again," I said. "If you gave me $5,000, do you think the pain of it potentially going down to $4,900 is greater than the potential for it to go up to $5,300?"

I could see her working it out, then she shut her eyes and put her hands over them. "No. No. The idea of losing money for school in the stock market makes me want to vomit."

"Why is that?" I asked.

"Because I need that money. Every dollar that it could drop down is a dollar I'll have to put on debt, and I bet I'd pay more in interest on that debt than I could earn in the market."

I nodded and smiled. "That is bang on," I said. "Your student debt could be at a rate of 6–9% depending on whatever the Bank of Canada sets the overnight rates as. That's guaranteed. Debt always charges interest. No matter what. But investment returns are not guaranteed. There's volatility. Historically, maybe the investment you chose went down for a bit but over the long run went up by 6–9%. That's great, but we can't know when and how that happens."

"So, the more I need the money, the less I should invest."

"Yep. It's something called your risk tolerance combined with your time horizon. Two very important investing concepts."

I could hear her tapping on her keyboard, writing it down.

"What are they?" she asked.

"Your time horizon is the length of time until you need the money. School is a short-term time horizon because you'll need it in one to two years. None of it is long-term time horizon."

"Would a long-term time horizon be money I saved for retirement one day? Or a down payment or something?"

"Long-term time horizon is money that you don't need for three or more years, preferably even five or more. Since investments have volatility, it's okay if your money goes down in the short run because it's likely that, over the long run, history will repeat itself, and the markets will rebound and go up."

"But if I needed the money, I'd be forced to take it out when the money is down. Like, I don't have time to wait until it bounces back."

"Exactly."

"So, I have a short risk tolerance."

"You have a short time horizon," I corrected. "Your risk tolerance is your ability to handle the lows that can come with investing. Think of it like a roller coaster, with some scary parts. Overall, it could be really fun, but how do you handle the scary parts? Are you like, 'Get me off this ride,' or can you breathe through it?"

She laughed. "I love Drop Zone."

"Then maybe you have a high risk tolerance! With investments, though, it's more about how much money you could lose before you'd be losing sleep."

"Oh." She sat back, thinking. "Again, with the money for school, I can't risk anything. Not even a dollar. Maybe later, I'll have more risk tolerance because I don't need the money right away to keep me out of debt."

I nodded. "Right now, with the money you have saved up, your risk tolerance is low and your time horizon is short. So we shouldn't invest the money."

She looked very disappointed. "You're saying that, because I need the money, I can't grow the money?"

"Not necessarily," I assured her. "There's still good old boring high-interest savings accounts that would maybe be the best place for your savings right now."

"Boring high interest, like compound interest?"

"Exactly."

"Right, right. I think we learned about that in school."

"Amazing, because the money for your school is a perfect candidate for it. The interest on your savings should keep pace with inflation, growing your money slowly, but with no risk of it going down at all."

"That feels right." I heard her clicking around again. "I'm on a website right now that sort of aggregates all the interest rates in Canada. Like, who's offering the best interest rate."

She shared her screen. I saw all the different financial institutions listing their high-interest savings account offerings and GICs.

"The GICs are higher than the savings accounts," she said. "Why wouldn't I do a GIC? There's a one-year GIC for 5%. That's amazing, right?"

"Good question. That is a great rate because interest rates and inflation are so high right now. GICs and high-interest-rate accounts are trying to keep your money in pace with inflation. Not necessarily beat it."

"But, if inflation is high right now, shouldn't my money go there to grow at the highest interest rate, with no risk of it going down?"

"For sure, but GICs can be tricky. With your savings plan, you're saving $1,870 each month, and you'll need most of that in a year or less. You'd almost have to start a new GIC each month. The first month, $1,870 in a one-year GIC. The second month, you would start a new GIC but you couldn't lock it in for 11 months because they don't come like that. So maybe you'd have to do nine months, and do the same the next month."

She nodded. "Ohhh, I see. So I'd have to have, like, a million GICs."

"Probably 12 times per year, but yes. It's a lot. Plus, the money is locked into the GIC so if you need to take any out for any reason, you'd lose the interest."

"They seem good if you have a chunk of money already saved up," she said.

"Exactly. If you already had your money saved up, a one-year GIC could be amazing."

"What about these high-interest savings accounts then," she asked, scanning the page on her screen. "This one here is highest—5%! Oh wait, but only for three months." She scanned again. "Oh here! This one is 4%. But, like, I've never even heard of this bank before."

I nodded.

"Is that sketchy?" she asked. "Like, what if that bank goes bank-rupt?"

"This is a wonderful, wonderful question, Tania. Do you see at the bottom there, where it says insurance: CDIC?"

I saw her highlight it with her mouse. "Yep."

"That's the most important thing for you to watch for when it comes to opening a high-interest savings account or GIC. It stands for Canadian Deposit Insurance Corp."*

"Insurance, like, if the bank goes bankrupt, I get some money back?"

"Essentially, yes! The CDIC is a federal Crown corporation that will automatically cover your holdings up to a certain amount if a finan-cial institution fails. Which is extremely rare in Canada. But, just in case. It's a sleep-at-night factor."

"Wow, amazing. So if the financial institution is CDIC eligible, that means it's one of the members, and therefore I don't have to worry about it going bankrupt even if I've never heard of the bank?"

"They cover up to $100,000 per person per account. For your school savings, that would be under the $100,000 cap, so yes, you'd be covered automatically as long as the financial institution was a CDIC member."

"That's exciting!"

"Absolutely," I said. I could tell she was extremely jazzed.

"How much extra money will I get on my $1,870 a month before school starts if I put it in at 4%?"

"It's calculated as 4% per year. So, it's 4% divided by 12 months or 0.33% per month."

I stopped her from sharing her screen and shared mine. "See? In one year, you'll have earned an extra $411.79 in interest!"

"Okay," she said. It was disappointment mixed with happiness.

"I know. I bet you wish it was more."

TIMELIME (MM-YY)	BEGINNING MONTH BALANCE	MONTHLY PAYMENT	INTEREST EARNED	ADDITIONAL MONTHLY SAVINGS	END OF MONTH BALANCE
JULY	0.00	0.00	0.00	1,870.00	$1,870.00
AUG	$1,870.00	$0.00	6.17	1,870.00	$3,746.17
SEPT	$3,746.17	$0.00	12.36	1,870.00	$5,628.53
OCT	$5,628.53	$0.00	18.57	1,870.00	$7,517.10
NOV	$7,517.10	$0.00	24.81	1,870.00	$9,411.91
DEC	$9,411.91	$0.00	31.06	1,870.00	$11,312.97
JAN	$11,312.97	$0.00	37.33	1,870.00	$13,220.30
FEB	$13,220.30	$0.00	43.63	1,870.00	$15,133.93
MAR	$15,133.93	$0.00	49.94	1,870.00	$17,053.87
APRIL	$17,053.87	$0.00	56.28	1,870.00	$18,980.15
MAY	$18,980.15	$0.00	62.63	1,870.00	$20,912.78
JUNE	$20,912.78	$0.00	69.01	1,870.00	$22,851.79

"I do."

"But hey, this is only 12 months. You can see how much more interest per month happens once you get some savings under your belt. Much of good finances is the long game. It takes patience."

"True, true." She thought for a moment, and then a big smile spread across her face. "You know what? $411 is $411. That's $411 I didn't have before."

"That's the spirit!"

"I'm going to open this account tonight. And one for travel."

I beamed. "I'm thrilled for you."

She did a bit of a happy dance, and we sat quietly for a moment. I knew once the call was over, I wouldn't talk to her for a long time.

"You should be so proud of yourself, Tania," I said. "You're doing it. You're doing it all."

"Thank you," she said. "For everything. Thank you so much."

"Tania, it has been an absolute pleasure helping you get this all set up. It's all you. All I did was tell you how to do it, you're the one that's actually doing the work. The hard work."

"Well, you know," she said, a bit bashful.

"You've got the skills to go so far in life. You're learning them and practising them now so that once you graduate, the world is your oyster."

"I'll call you. We can get into all that investment stuff once I'm done with school and have a job."

"I'd love that."

I can't wait to see the email from Tania in a few years from now. There is no doubt in my mind that this young woman will pay for school, be debt-free, travel, get the job of her dreams, and save for the next big things in her life.

GO, TANIA, GO!

CHAPTER 18 NITTY GRITTY

What Is the Canadian Deposit Insurance Corporation (CDIC)?

- The CDIC is a Crown corporation that will protect your money if the bank goes bankrupt.

- It's very important to check that savings and chequing accounts are CDIC insured.

- You can read more about how much is covered here: https://www.cdic.ca/depositors/whats-covered/.

19

Mia, Who Is Hopeful for Her Financial Future

AGE:	13
SIBLING STATUS:	Middle kid between two sisters
INCOME SOURCE:	Has a regular allowance
CURRENT SAVINGS:	$60

At our meeting after the grad dance, Mia had asked me one of the hardest questions ever when it comes to money.

"But what happens if you actually can't afford anything?" she asked. "Like, if you are actually broke? How do you grow your money so you can afford to have a bit of fun and pay for your life?"

I let out a big sigh. "This is a big question."

Mia widened her eyes. "Please don't tell me it's impossible to have fun and pay for your life."

"Of course not. But the truth is, there's no magical way to grow your money. There isn't some investment where you put your money in and it's guaranteed to double the next day. If there were, everyone would do it and no one would work."

She paused, looked at the door to ensure her mom couldn't hear, and then whispered, "My friend's older sister made a lot of money on game stocks."

"Game stocks?" I said, confused.

"During a pandemic lockdown. She bought some shares. Lots of shares of this video game company and made thousands, like, overnight."

"Oh!" I said.

She nodded enthusiastically but was still quiet. "Yeah. She pretty much paid for her entire first year at school. Or at least, that's what my friend said."

"Is she, the sister who invested, the legal age to invest?"

"Yeah," she whispered.

"Why are you whispering?" I whispered back.

She smiled mischievously and leaned in. "My friend says her sister would invest my money in her account, and I can buy whatever stocks I want. Me and my friend. If we need to make some serious money, fast."

"Oh," I said. "Oh, I see."

She sat back. "Is that something I should do? I could definitely use thousands of dollars overnight." Her eyes almost sparkled at the mention of it.

"Let me start by saying that I do not think this is a good idea for a few reasons."

She scrunched up her face in a fake pout. "I thought you'd say that."

"Then you asked because you don't really want to do this. If you did, you probably would have gone ahead and not bothered asking if I thought it was a good idea."

"You're good."

"Listen, I'm all for experimenting with our finances and having fun with it, but let me tell you why I don't think betting all your savings on a single stock is a good idea."

"Okay." She sighed. "Because honestly, the idea of a quick thousand is really appealing."

I held my hand up. "The idea of a quick thousand is not real. It's a fantasy that only a few people ever actually get to realize. It's, like, an investing urban legend."

"What do you mean? This actually happened to my friend's older sister. Like, I know her."

"Totally. But lucky windfalls are the exception, not the rule. The point is that most investments don't work like that, and when people put all their savings into one stock trying to win big in a short period of time, it can be very risky. I've seen people lose so much money this way."

"So, are those bad investments?"

"No, it's not about bad investments or good investments or a specific stock. It's *bad* because they put all their money into one investment that could be very volatile. I would be worried about anyone taking all their savings and putting it into any stock. I'd even be worried if someone took their life savings and put it all into one reliable stock. It doesn't matter the stock. That's a risky move because it's not diversified."

"Diversified is what?" she asked.

"Sorry. Jargon. Diversified investments are when you spread your savings out across a number of different investments or stocks. Essentially, the opposite of 'putting all your eggs in one basket.' This way, if one stock or investment goes down, you have money in a whole bunch of them so the risk of losing everything at once goes way down."

"Oh, I get it. You're saying my friend's sister, the one who made thousands, got lucky because the way she invested was risky, not necessarily the stock."

"That's exactly what I'm saying. With investing, you always want to ensure three things. First, that the money you're investing can handle some ups and downs. That's called volatility."

She looked at me and I could tell she was doing the nod-along thing.

"Okay, okay," I said, "look at this." I pulled up a chart of the stock market from 2004 to 2014. "This is the Toronto Stock Exchange* from 2004 to 2014."

"That's old," she said with a laugh.

"Ancient," I agreed. "But this decade shows something really important. See the big drop in the middle in 2008?"

She nodded.

"I like that the 2008 crash is right in the middle because it shows some investment basics. Have you heard of the Great Recession in 2008?" I asked.

"My mom talks about it all the time. She lost so much money in her retirement accounts."

"I didn't know your mom then, but I wonder if she lost it all forever or maybe gained it back."

Her back straightened right up. "Wait, you can gain money back after you lose it? That doesn't make sense."

"You absolutely can, but over time. Have a look."

I pulled out a piece of paper and started to draw a dotted line with a marker. "Stocks go up and down. It's called volatility."

I drew a line that mimicked the ups and downs of the Toronto Stock Exchange Composite Index over the 10-year period.*

She leaned over to see my drawing.

"This drawing is just to illustrate the nature of volatility, okay? The nature of stocks versus bonds."

She nodded.

"See how the dotted line goes up, then down a bit, then up again, then down again, and then—" I drew a big V. "There's this big drop. This would be a major recession. Like the 2008 one."

She nodded again, and I think she got it.

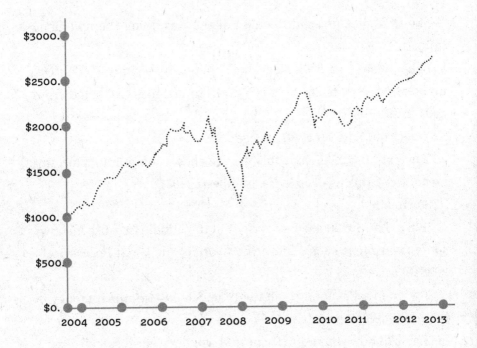

"Imagine, in our example here, that in 2004, you invested $1,000, put it all in Canadian stocks. In 2007, you would likely have doubled your money! But then the crash happened." I traced my finger from the top of my drawing to the bottom dramatically. "Boom. You lost all those gains."

"But not the initial $1,000," she said.

"No, but all the money from investing. Over three years."

"Ouch."

"Ouch," I echoed. "But here's the thing, if you didn't need the money in 2008 for retirement, or to buy a house, or whatever, and you could stay invested and wait it out, look what happens in 2009."

I drew a dotted line that mimicked the year-over-year returns of the Toronto Stock Exchange from 2009 to 2012.

"It came back up," she said.

"It came back up. Because you didn't panic-sell at the bottom of the market." I pointed to the bottom of the big V.

"So when people say they lost money, they haven't really lost it if it's still invested?"

"That's right! While it's invested no one has actually made money or lost money because it could change tomorrow."

"Right. If my friend's older sister hadn't cashed out at the top and had stayed invested instead, she wouldn't have actually made as much. Because the stock went back down."

"Exactly."

"And you're saying all investments go up and down. Some more than others."

"Yes. As soon as you invest, there's volatility—that's the ups and downs because your money is not in a high-interest savings account or GIC. With stocks and bonds, there are ups and downs. That's normal and part of investing. Hopefully more ups than downs. Historically, that's been the case."

"I wonder if my mom waited it out or sold?"

"You should ask her."

"I will." She looked again at the chart. "So what about bonds?"

I opened up the historical return data for a Canadian Aggregate Bond Index* and drew a solid line on the same graph with my drawing of the Canadian stock market, then held it out to her (see graph on next page).

"They don't go up or down as much as the stocks. Why?" she asked.

"Typically, bonds are less volatile than stocks. They go up and down but, historically, not as much as stocks." I traced my finger over the solid line. "I like to think of bonds like having your parents at a high school party."

She burst out laughing, "What?"

"When times are good, a.k.a. the stock market is going up, it's easy to resent the bonds you have in your well-diversified portfolio because they aren't typically going up as much as the stocks. Kind of

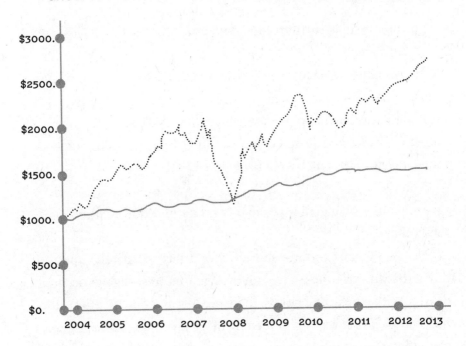

a drag. So, at a high school party, you may resent having your parents around because they make it feel less awesome during the good times. But, if the party gets crashed, parents will hopefully make sure not as much damage happens."

"I'd be like, thank God those bonds are there!"

"Exactly! Historically speaking."

"Is it always like that? Stocks go up, bonds don't do much. Stocks go down, bonds go up or hold?"

I shook my head. "Nothing with investing is 'always,' or guaranteed. We just look to the past and try to use that to make informed decisions. That's why diversification is so, so important. Because no one has a crystal ball."

She looked at my drawing. "Wait. I have a question."

"Lay it on me."

"What if I put in all my money in here?" She pointed to the peak of the dotted line just before the crash.

"Great observation! And your intuition is bang on. If you invested $2,300 in there, like the people in 2007, within a year, you'd have lost more than half the money."

"That would have sucked."

"Yes," I said.

"I guess this is like when people buy a trending stock after it's already gone way, way up. They buy in right at the top and then it can crash?"

I nodded. "That happens."

"And I guess if you're buying a stock, trying to get rich overnight, you're not waiting it out five years to make your money back?"

"Exactly. That's what makes it luck opposed to good investing. If you got in and out at the right time that was lucky. Not a solid investment strategy that paid off."

Her finger traced the dotted line on the drawing. "So the 2007 people who could wait it out and not sell when they were down, they would have made it back to the initial amount of money after a few years."

I nodded. "Yep. That's what happened to me. Personally. It was really scary."

"You?" she asked, surprised.

"Yes! I had just graduated and opened my first RRSP account, and I was saving money. My first taste of investing was the 2008/2009 Great Recession. It was hard to stay in and have faith that things would come back up. But they did."

"Oh my God. That sounds so scary."

"It was, but also the best lesson in risk tolerance for me personally."

She sat back for a moment. "So basically, investment markets can be bumpy sometimes, but in the end, they hopefully go up? That's, like, the whole point?"

I nodded. "Well, that's the whole point and the hope. But again, nothing is guaranteed. What's likely is not the same as a guarantee."

She nodded. "Hence the diversification?"

"You got it."

"You want some parents at the high school party," she said with a laugh. "Enough that you're not terrified, but not so many that you're not having fun. And you also want a bunch of different types of people there. Both high school students and adults. A diverse group."

"Precisely. The jargon way of saying that is that 'you want a well-diversified portfolio with an asset mix—bonds and stocks—that suits your risk tolerance and time horizon, and then you want to ensure that the equity portion of your portfolio is also well diversified.'"

Her eyes went wide, and she shook her head. "That's a mouthful."

I laughed. "It is. But I think you actually get it."

"I think I do too! But I don't think I can do any of this until I'm 18."

"Correct. You have to wait."

She let out a fake exasperated sigh, then dramatically said, "Is everything with money about waiting?"

"Yes! So much of money is about the long game. Slow and steady wins the race. No quick fixes. No get-rich-quick. Nothing is instant."

She gave a funny dissatisfied look at this.

"The good news is that now you know how to track, save, and spend. You can practise all these habits now, and when you're older, saving and living within your means will be second nature."

"Then I can invest." She tapped her fingers together, pretending to be scheming, looking devious.

"Then you can invest in a well-balanced, low-fee, diversified portfolio. Yes."

"Not taking my investing advice from random folks on the internet?"

"The internet has a lot of wonderful information out there. But also, a lot of unhelpful information. You need to make sure the people you're following are reputable."

"No get-rich-quick meme-stocks?"

"Not unless the meme is that investing is a long game of a well-balanced, low-fee, diversified portfolio when you have a long-term time horizon."

She sighed. "So, you mean boring."

"Absolutely," I said proudly. "So much of good common sense with money is boring. I've been doing this a long time. Often those with the most boring strategies end up the richest in the end."

She nodded. "In the end. And for now, I just focus on earning my money, saving my money, and spending it on safe and happy things. Then I'll have all these good habits down for when I'm 18, and I can start to invest if it makes sense."

I clapped my hands. "Mia, I love it. I'm so happy your mom set this up. I wish all kids had a chance to learn these wonderful and boring money lessons as early as you."

"Not all of what you've taught me was actually boring. Just the investment stuff," she said with a grin.

I laughed.

"Maybe I can come back in a few years when I have a proper job and not just an allowance."

"If it's okay with your mom, I'd love that so much."

She gathered up her blue notebook and pen, and I opened the door. Sofia gave me a nod and a smile.

"It was such a pleasure to work with you, Mia," I said.

"Can I give you a hug?" she asked.

I opened my arms wide. "Please!"

We hugged and I could hear Sofia laughing.

"She wants to come back in a few years, Sofia," I said, grinning.

"So I can invest in the most boring way that will make me long-term rich," Mia said.

"I like that idea." Sofia put a hand on Mia's back. "I'm proud of you."

Mia blushed a bit.

"You should be. She's gonna do great." I looked at Mia. "Good luck with school, your allowance, your budget. All of it!"

"Thanks for everything, Shannon. I can't wait to show you all the money I've saved up in a few years!"

I put a hand over my heart. "I absolutely can't wait either."

Mia and Sofia left the office and I could hear them laughing as they walked down the hall. I had a smile on my face for the rest of the day.

CHAPTER 19 NITTY GRITTY

Where to Find Historical Investment Market Returns

- You can search on Yahoo Finance under Chart.

  - For Canada, you can use a S&P/TSX Composite Index or ETF.

  - For Bonds, you can use a Canadian Universe Bond Index or ETF.

Do You Know Your Stuff?

Test your knowledge with these True or False questions.

QUESTION 1: Diversified investments are when you spread your savings out across a number of different investments or stocks.

True.

QUESTION 2: Putting all your money in one stock is a great way to earn fast money.

False! This is very risky and can backfire and lose you money.

QUESTION 3: While money is invested, no one has actually made or lost money because it could change tomorrow. *True.*

QUESTION 4: Volatility is to be expected with investments. Nothing is guaranteed. *True.*

QUESTION 5: You want a well-diversified portfolio with an asset mix (bonds and stocks) that suits your risk tolerance and time horizon, and then you want to ensure that the equity portion of your portfolio is also well diversified. *True.*

HOMEWORK

If you're interested in learning more about investing, find three reputable Canadian-specific investment people whose social media, podcast, or newsletter you can follow. Here are some tips for choosing reputable people to follow:

1. Ensure they have proper credentials, for example, CFP, CIM, CFA.

2. Look up their professional experience.

3. Make sure they aren't trying to sell you their services.

You may not be old enough to invest yet, but if you are interested in learning more before you can start, make sure you're getting good information.

20

Oliver, Who Learned to Ask for What He Needs

AGE:	16
SIBLING STATUS:	Only child
INCOME SOURCE:	Has a regular allowance
REGULAR INCOME:	$150 a month from allowance
CURRENT SAVINGS:	$500 in an online chequing account; an RESP for university (if he gets in); a stock simulator account with $5,000 in it—Oliver makes stock trades to practise, then his dad executes the trades for real in an online investment account that Oliver will have access to when he's 18

Back to Oliver. I asked Oliver if there was anything else he wanted to ask about finances.

He looked at his dad. Then to me.

"Is crypto a good investment?"

"That's a doozy of a question," I said, smiling.

John cleared his throat. "I suspect this is directed at me because, well, I don't know if Oliver told you, but I have a sum of money put aside that I invest on his behalf. He gets to make the choices in a stock simulator account, and then I trade them in real time so that he gets to learn about investing, dividends, capital gains, et cetera."

"And cryptocurrency," I added with a grin.

John's eyes shot to Oliver and then back to me. "Yes. I also bought some cryptocurrency, and that didn't pan out as well as we'd hoped."

"As well as *you'd* hoped," Oliver corrected.

"Son, you were there and just as curious. I only traded that with your permission. I—"

"Dad, it's fine. I'm just razzing you." Oliver grinned.

John did not look like he appreciated the razzing. He adjusted himself in his seat, his face a little flushed.

"Oliver," I said, "do you actually want to know my opinions about crypto, or are you just putting your dad on the spot?"

Oliver put a hand on his heart and feigned shock. "I'm offended by that, Shannon. Of course I want to know if my future is blown because of a bad cryptocurrency purchase."

"That's enough," John said in a warning tone.

"I agree," I said.

Oliver held up his hands, like a peace offering. As if to say, "Okay, okay, I'll stop."

"John, can I ask," I started, "how much of the $5,000 you invest on Oliver's behalf was in the cryptocurrency?"

"We bought $500 near the end of 2021." He looked at me. Waiting for my reaction.

"A lot of people bought crypto for the first time in 2021," I said. "Some people have made lots of money, some people have lost lots of money."

"Yeah, well, we lost," Oliver said.

"What's it worth now?" I asked.

"About $350," John said.

"So, not a good investment," Oliver chimed in.

"Hold on," I said.

"Isn't that, like, a 30% loss, though?" Oliver asked, annoyed.

"It is, but it's also only been a year. It's not really a good idea to judge if something is a"—I made air quotes with my hands—"good investment' or a 'bad investment' after such a short time. I'd say the same thing if you purchased a blue-chip dividend stock that went down."

"Aren't blue-chip stocks* safe?" Oliver asked.

I sat back and eyed him for a moment. "What does 'safe' mean for you here?"

His eyes sort of widened. "Uh." He shrugged. "Like, not going to go down?"

I shook my head. "As soon as your money leaves high-interest savings accounts or Guaranteed Investment Certificates, it can go down. All investments have some type of volatility. If you want something that never goes down, you have to stick to things like high-interest savings accounts and GICs."

"But those have no opportunity for growth," John added. "They just keep pace with inflation. The entire point of investing is to grow your money *more* than inflation."

Oliver looked to me to confirm or deny this tidbit from his dad. I nodded. "Absolutely. And with that potential growth comes risk. Risk with investing doesn't mean risk like—oh, I don't know—perhaps the risk of gambling."

Neither of them laughed.

"Too soon?" I joked. "But I mean it. And I think we should discuss the difference. I would do this even if there were no such thing as sports betting."

"Yeah, right," Oliver mumbled.

"Oliver," I said earnestly, "I'm not taking a cheap shot. Truly, some people think investing is gambling. It's not at all, and it's important to understand the difference."

"Okay, fine," he said curtly.

I carried on. "Sometimes, when we talk about investing, we talk about this thing called the risk return trade-off. It's an investment

principle that basically says, the more risk you take, the more potential return you could get. The return is the money you make, or rather
the money you could make."

"Like slot machines," Oliver said. "If you play the penny slots, you
don't lose much money, but you're not going to gain much money
either. If you play the $5 slots, you could lose much more, but gain
much more."

I grimaced a bit at the gambling reference, given the circum-
stances, but he had a point. "That's a great point. But again, I am
careful not to compare gambling to investing."

"Gambling is irresponsible," John piped in. "Investing is smart."

"Investing can also be irresponsible," I said, and John flinched.
"When not done correctly or for the right reasons. Think about people who jumped on the bandwagon with those meme stocks and lost
thousands." I turned to Oliver. "Even though the stocks themselves
are not risky, jumping on a bandwagon based on a stock meme could
be very similar to gambling."

"Well, of course," John said. "If you're talking about throwing your
money at something trendy, yes."

"Plenty of people thought—and still think—crypto is trendy."

He was getting huffy. "I don't think that a $500 purchase of crypto
is the same as throwing your life savings at a meme stock."

"It's not. It's not the same at all. And that's the *exact* difference.
There are always going to be investment opportunities that are new
or alternative investments, or maybe a stock that could be extremely
volatile, which may give it an opportunity for big growth. A long shot.
Just because something is volatile, or risky, doesn't mean that it's bad
or irresponsible. An investment becomes irresponsible for two reasons." I counted them off on my fingers. "First, when someone invests
money they'll need within the next one to two years."

I waited for them to nod along.

"And second, when they invest in something that is potentially extremely volatile with an amount of money that they can't actually afford to lose."

"Like life savings on a stock tip type thing," Oliver said.

"Exactly," I said. "For you, putting $500 into crypto to see what happens and taking a long shot is not irresponsible because it's a small portion of what you have. You don't need the money in the next one to two years, so you have a long time horizon. Plus, it's an amount of money that, even if it went to zero, you'd all still be financially okay."

"But if we YOLO'd the full $5,000, that would be irresponsible," Oliver said.

"Yes." Noticing John looking confused, I added, "By YOLO, I know you mean if you put your entire savings into a single high-risk investment."

"People do that, you know." Oliver said it almost like a challenge. I think he was testing to see if I knew about these types of online investing threads on social media. "They post their trades online. They trade, like, thousands and try to double it."

I said nothing.

He shrugged. "Sometimes it works," he said in a tone that was far too nonchalant for me.

"And many times, it doesn't." I leaned in and was very serious. "Oliver, this is not a safe or smart way to grow your money. Anybody's money," I added in a warning tone. "YOLOing with your money is almost like gambling."

"Buy high, sell low," he said with a giggle.

"That's where it leaves a lot of people," I said solemnly.

John chimed in. "What are you two talking about?"

I looked to John. "Online investing threads on social media that glorify massive losses and taking huge risks. We all know that the point of investing is to buy low and sell high. There's a thread online that makes a joke about the massive losses people end up with because many people buy when a stock is high, or it's a risky long-shot, and they end up losing everything."

Oliver was quiet, but he had a smile. I was not impressed.

"It's not funny," I said to him, so seriously that he stopped smiling. "I've seen this ruin people's lives and marriages. Someone losing their life savings isn't funny."

"No, I know that," Oliver said defensively. "But, like, they made the trade." He held his hands up, as if to say, "It's their fault."

"Why would anyone do that?" John asked. "Throw money away like that?"

"I can only speak to what I've seen. Most times, it comes from a desperate place. People feel like no matter how hard they work, they will never be able to get ahead, so they feel they have to take these massive risks with their money to 'get lucky.'"

"That's quite upsetting," John said.

"It is," I agreed. "It's one thing to take some of the money that you can afford to lose, that could go to zero, and take a flyer. It's quite another to publicly post your entire life savings going into one single stock on the off chance you get lucky. That's why investing like that is akin to gambling. It can start a loss cycle where you bet bigger and bigger, trying to cover the last loss."

"I didn't think about it like that," Oliver mumbled sheepishly. "It just seemed funny online."

I let the silence sit for a moment. Awkward silence can be very effective.

Oliver spoke first. "So, what you're saying is, my dad and I should combine our money and invest everything tomorrow into one long-shot penny stock,* yeah?"

We all laughed and the tension was broken. "Very funny," I said.

"I know you're joking," John said to Oliver. "But I also need to know that you don't think this 'YOLOing the market' is a good idea, right?"

"No," Oliver said. "Unless it was an amount of money that could safely go to zero."

I smiled. "Exactly. Money that you can afford to go to zero."

"Who can afford play money these days?" John asked incredulously. "In this economy?"

"Not many people," I said. "Which is why it's scary when you see it."

"So, do we just keep on investing the way we are?" John asked.

"I would start by looking at Oliver's risk tolerance." I turned to him. "I'd say your tolerance is very high. You are not afraid of volatility in exchange for potential high returns."

"That's true," Oliver agreed, proudly.

"Plus, your time horizon is long for this $5,000. You don't plan to spend it or use it for five years or more, right? Even past 18 years old?"

"That's right," John said.

I looked at Oliver to confirm. "Yeah?"

He nodded.

"So, the fact that you're invested in blue-chip stocks and well diversified with exchange-traded funds,* I'd say it's a well-balanced, low-fee, diversified portfolio that suits your time horizon and risk tolerance." I was smiling.

"And that's good," Oliver said.

"That's great," I said.

"Good," John said. I could tell he felt vindicated.

"And if I want to invest in something high risk when I turn 18," Oliver said, "I can just invest with an amount of money I'm okay with totally losing."

"Oliver, no," John said. "That's—"

I cut him off gently by raising my hand.

"It will be his money then, right?"

John nodded.

"So, Oliver, you can absolutely do that," I said. "The key is not to 'YOLO.' Don't throw in your life savings. Only play high risk with an amount that you can afford to fully lose."

"You think it's okay for him to lose money?" John said, genuinely shocked.

I leaned forward. "John, I know it's not conventional thinking, but I believe it can be a great way for people to truly learn their risk tolerance. It's one thing to sit here and say, 'I have a high risk tolerance. I can handle ups and downs.' It's entirely another thing to watch your money go down. It's hard. With a little bit of *safe* experimentation, we scratch that itch on the rebellious side of us, or the overly optimistic side that hopes for a big break, and we can learn who we really are when it comes to investment losses."

Oliver spoke up. "It's a problem only if I start using money that I can't afford to lose."

"Exactly. Money for bills and spending money. Money for responsible short- and long-term savings. Those all come first. And if you actually have money left over after filling all those buckets, congrats! That's no easy feat. Especially these days."

They both nodded, and we didn't say anything else. It felt like we had said it all.

John looked at the clock and stood up. "We've taken a lot of your time. Thank you so much for today." We shook hands.

"It was lovely to meet you."

"I'll wait outside," John said to Oliver, and he walked out the door.

I turned to Oliver and released a big sigh. "I can't wait to see how you make your first million."

"Well, it won't be from YOLOing or sports betting," he said with a smile.

"Good," I said. "Do you feel good about everything? The allowance? The plan? All of it?"

He smiled and nodded. "The allowance will be a game changer."

"I think so too."

He got up and put his backpack on. "Thank you."

"No, Oliver, thank you."

"This would be an exciting chapter in your book," he joked.

"Oh, Oliver, this is going to be the entire book!"

We laughed hard.

"You stay in touch, okay? Call me for some financial planning when you're grown-up."

"I will."

I was going to miss him. I was worried about him. I knew, deep down, he was going to be okay. He might take some time to find his footing and do things his way, but he was smart and resourceful, and those aren't just good money skills, they are good life skills. Besides, he was young and time was on his side. Like it is for you!

CHAPTER 20 NITTY GRITTY

Blue-Chip Stock
This is a stock in a company that is well-established. The company has likely been around for a long time and has a good reputation for operating at a profit in good times and bad times.

Penny Stock
This is stock in a company that has a low price (below $5 per share). It is usually very speculative. Penny stocks are often considered high risk because they are speculative, potentially have lots of volatility, and often can't be sold easily.

Exchange-Traded Funds (ETFs)
This is a group of securities (stocks or bonds) that are pooled together to trade on the stock exchange. Many times, ETFs attempt to copy a specific index.

Do You Know Your Stuff?
Test your knowledge with these True or False questions.

QUESTION 1: The risk return trade-off says "the less risk you take, the more potential return you could get."

False. The risk return trade-off says "the *more* risk you take, the more potential return you could get."

QUESTION 2: You should never invest in a long-shot stock or an alternative investment.

False. It can be okay to experiment with a long-shot stock or alternative investment. However, only invest an amount of money that you do not need in the short term and that you can afford to have go to zero and still be financially secure.

QUESTION 3: The point of investing is to beat inflation. *True.*

QUESTION 4: A loss cycle is where you bet bigger and bigger, trying to cover the last loss. *True.*

QUESTION 5: Scared money doesn't make money.

False! Investing so that the investments you hold match your risk tolerance is very important. Do not take on additional risk beyond what you're comfortable with.

HOMEWORK

1. Set up an online stock market simulator account and invest in three different things:

   • A stock from a company

   • An exchange-traded fund for a country

   • A bond from a company

2. Over the next 30 days, journal about the following:

   • Did you get excited when your investments went up?

   • Did you get nervous when they went down?

   • Did you second-guess your choices?

   • Along the way, did you want to change your investment choices?

Conclusion

You did it! Congrats! If you're reading this, it means you are wise beyond your years. You have just read a book that, I hope, will set you up for a lifetime of financial success.

You know how to track your money, no matter how you make it. You know how to project it into the future so you can make plans.

You know how to set savings targets for short-term and long-term savings. You know why both are important.

You know how to make a budget and spend money within your means so that you don't wind up in a debt loop.

You know how to have a good relationship with money and why that matters.

Lastly, you know how to grow your money one day so that all the effort you put into tracking, saving, and spending can pay off!

No one knows exactly what the future holds. We don't have a crystal ball, but that doesn't need to be scary. No matter how the world changes, you are prepared. You've got the skills, and you can start practising them tomorrow.

I'm so excited for you. Good luck. You got this!

XO,
Shannon

Acknowledgements

have many people to thank for this book. This book would not be possible without the following people, and I'm so grateful! THANK YOU, THANK YOU, THANK YOU!

Mom—My fourth book and the fourth time you're listed as my number one thank-you. Thank you for being my sounding board, my brainstormer, my you-can-do-this don't-quit cheerleader. None of my books, including this one, would ever have happened without your endless support and guidance. You must live forever, Fan.

Matt—My fourth book and the fourth time I cannot thank you enough for being the most amazing partner. I love you. I am able to be a mom, run a business, and write books because we have such good teamwork and you're always in my corner. You always support me on whatever Capricorn deadline roller coaster I put myself on. Thanks for loving me just the way I am.

My family—Thank you again for your continued love and support. Whether it's taking my kids for the weekend so I can write, babysitting so I can have a break, or listening to me talk through the same book-writing drama over and over, I am so grateful and feel lucky to have such a cozy family and extended family.

My friends—Thanks for being there for late-night (or early morning) neighbourhood walks, giggles, long phone calls, floats in the "grotto," writing weekends away, and good cheer when I feel overwhelmed by all the things I need to get done. I love you all.

My team at the New School of Finance Inc.—Thank you for always holding down the fort when I need to switch into book mode and take way too long to respond to internal emails. I know that I could not do this without such a supportive, smart, dedicated team that understands how I work and laughs along with me. How did I get so lucky? Thank you so much.

Cindy Nguyen—Thank you so much for the help and support in reaching community youth groups and having the opportunity to learn from them for this book.

Laura Ball—Thank you for endless education about education and for translating slang that made me feel old. ☺

Mike Hook—Thank you for your help navigating the world of contract law.

Ashley Gordon, Alexandra Macqueen, and the FP Canada team—Thank you for helping me realistically ground these stories in the wonderful and important world of financial planning in Canada.

My editor, Yash Kesanakurthy—Thank you for your trust in me for this wonderful project. Thank you for your keen eye and enthusiasm. This book wouldn't be what it is without you.

My agent, Martha Webb—Thank you for being awesome. You are the cornerstone of any writing dream team.

HarperCollins Canada—Thank you again for the opportunity to write something important and put it out into the world. I'm grateful.